BUDDHA ŚĀKYAMUNI

Guru Padmasambhava

༄༅། །པདྨ་མཁའ་འགྲོའི་ཐུགས་ཐིག་ལས། རྫོགས་པ་ཆེན་པོ་སེམས་ཉིད་རང་གྲོལ་གྱི་རྒྱུད་ཀྱི་ རྩ་བ་དང་ཁང་སར་རིན་པོ་ཆེ་བསྟན་པའི་དབང་ ཕྱུག་གིས་མཛད་པའི་འགྲེལ་པ་ཡེ་ཤེས་ འོད་སྣང་ཞེས་བྱ་བ་བཞུགས། །

པདྨ་ཀཱ་རའི་སྒྲ་བསྒྱུར་མཐུན་ཚོགས་ནས་
སྒྲ་བསྒྱུར་ཞུས།།

The Padmakara Translation Group gratefully acknowledges the generous support of the Tsadra Foundation in sponsoring the translation and preparation of this book.

KHANGSAR TENPA'I WANGCHUK'S COLLECTED WORKS

The Natural Openness and Freedom of the Mind

A Treasure Tantra of the Great Perfection

Deshek Lingpa

WITH A COMMENTARY BY
Khangsar Tenpa'i Wangchuk

TRANSLATED BY THE
Padmakara Translation Group

SHAMBHALA

Shambhala Publications, Inc.
2129 13th Street
Boulder, Colorado 80302
www.shambhala.com

9 8 7 6 5 4 3 2 1

First Edition
Printed in the United States of America

Shambhala Publications makes every effort to print on acid-free, recycled paper. For more information please visit www.shambhala.com.

Shambhala Publications is distributed worldwide by Penguin Random House, Inc., and its subsidiaries.

LIBRARY OF CONGRESS CATALOGING-IN-PUBLICATION DATA
Names: Lingpa, Deshek, author. | Bstan-pa'i-dbang-phyug, Khang-sar
Rin-po-che Dbon-sprul, 1938–2014 | Comité de traduction Padmakara,
translator.
Title: The natural openness and freedom of the mind: a treasure tantra
of the great perfection / Deshek Lingpa with a commentary by Khangsar
Tenpa'i Wangchuk; translated by the Padmakara Translation Group.
Description: First edition. | Boulder: Shambhala, 2024. |
Includes bibliographical references and index.
Identifiers: LCCN 2023041895 | ISBN 9781645473343 (hardcover;
acid-free paper)
Subjects: Rdzogs-chen. | Rnying-ma-pa (Sect)—Doctrines. |
Spiritual life—Buddhism.
Classification: LCC BQ7662.4 .L56 2024 | DDC 294.3/85--dc23/
eng/20240126
LC record available at https://lccn.loc.gov/2023041895

Contents

FOREWORD

When, in the autumn of 2019, Khangsar Tenpa'i Wangchuk's nephew and lineage holder, Tsultrim Zangpo Rinpoche, kindly took the long journey to come to France to transmit his uncle's teachings in fulfillment of a prediction that they would be propagated in the West, I felt particularly fortunate, for from the moment my brother Pema Wangyal Rinpoche and I heard about Tenpa'i Wangchuk and his commentary on Longchenpa's *Precious Treasury of the Dharmadhātu*, we both felt a deep yearning to receive his teaching and blessing. I was delighted when Tenpa'i Wangchuk's student Yingrik Drubpa Rinpoche and Pema Wangyal Rinpoche arranged for these transmissions to be given in Dordogne. In his biography we read that Tenpa'i Wangchuk had direct visions of buddhas and bodhisattvas, ḍākas and ḍākinīs, and wisdom Dharma protectors. We can therefore be sure that his teachings are fully authentic. They are, moreover, expressed in clear, simple language that makes even the most profound and detailed subjects directly accessible.

The occasion of those transmissions also marked the beginning of a project to translate Tenpa'i Wangchuk's Collected Works into English and other Western languages, which Tsultrim Zangpo Rinpoche and Yingrik Drubpa Rinpoche have graciously entrusted to the Padmakara Translation Group. The first of these works, a commentary on *The Precious Treasury of the Fundamental Nature*, has already been published, and the second is now complete: his commentary on a Dzogchen tantra. As Tenpa'i Wangchuk has written, this Great Perfection teaching *The Natural Openness and Freedom of the Mind* is like the heart essence of the vidyādhara Garab Dorje, the great founder and charioteer of the Great Perfection. Garab Dorje bestowed it on the sublime teacher of the profound secret mantras, Śrīsiṃha, who gave it as an instruction to the son of the conquerors, Padmasambhava. The latter entrusted it to his wisdom consort, the lady of Kharchen, the ḍākinī Yeshe Tsogyal. The ḍākinī made inconceivable aspirations that it would benefit the beings of later generations afflicted by the five degenerations and sealed it with seven immutable seals inside the precious casket of the expanse of her disciple Yudra Nyingpo's mind. And it was an emanation of the latter, Padmasambhava's regent, the great treasure revealer Deshek Lingpa, who, in order to bring to maturity the mindstreams of fortunate disciples in future generations, revealed this tantra from the secret treasure of his mind. He subsequently appointed Khangsar Tenpa'i Wangchuk as the holder of this profound teaching and, presenting him with many auspicious materials, asked him to write a commentary on it.

As Tenpa'i Wangchuk points out, this tantra is the quintessence of the subtle essence of the great master Padmasambhava's mind. It is a profound pith instruction, like blood that is the vital essence of the heart of the hundred thousand ḍākinīs of the mother tantras. And it is the very quintessence of Deshek Lingpa's mind treasures. Moreover, it includes in a single stream the teachings of the three profound Heart Essences, and thus it gathers into one the treasures of the hundred great treasure revealers. Yet compared to them, there is none more profound than this tantra.

We are immensely fortunate to have received the blessings of the lineage from Tsultrim Zangpo Rinpoche and to be able to read this text. And we feel doubly fortunate now in being able to present this translation to readers in the West. Those who have the fortune to read it can consider that they are exposed to the profound blessings of Guru Padmasambhava and Khandro Yeshe Tsogyal. For as we read in the concluding verses,

> All living beings without exception
> Who see, hear, think of it, or touch it
> Will soon attain buddhahood
> As the children of the conquerors.

Wherever this teaching is present,
All illnesses and misfortunes will be cleared away;
Long life, good health, and well-being
Will prevail throughout the land.

I feel immense gratitude to Khangsar Tenpa'i Wangchuk and his lineage holders, and to the translators, publishers, and generous sponsors, and I pray that this may indeed come true.

Jigme Khyentse
July, 2023

SERIES INTRODUCTION

The Collected Works of Khangsar Tenpa'i Wangchuk (1938–2014) bears eloquent testimony to the continuance in Tibet, despite the immense difficulties endured since the Chinese invasion in the 1950s, of the literary tradition of original texts and commentaries composed by Tibetan masters over the past fourteen centuries. The writings of this great contemporary scholar are all the more remarkable for including not only works on Indian and Tibetan classics but also unprecedented commentaries on two of Kunkhyen Longchenpa's Seven Treasuries, the first, within the Tibetan lineage, to be written by anyone other than Longchenpa himself, six centuries earlier.[1]

A detailed biography of the author is included in the first volume of his Collected Works. For the present purposes, that of introducing the series generally, the salient details of his remarkable life may be briefly reviewed as follows. Khangsar Khenpo Tenpa'i Wangchuk was born in the Akyong Khangsar district of Golok, a remote region of Eastern Tibet now included in the Chinese administrative province of Qinghai. Not long after his birth, he was recognized by important lamas of different schools as the rebirth of Panak Öntrul Rigdzin Dorje, an emanation of Yudra Nyingpo, a disciple of the great eighth-century translator Vairotsana, and one of the twenty-five principal disciples of Guru Padmasambhava. He received his first monastic ordination in 1952 at the age of fourteen from Akyong Khenpo Lozang Dorje of the Payul tradition. Affiliated as he therefore was to the Nyingma school, in the years that followed, Tenpa'i Wangchuk received a rigorous education that was strongly marked by the nonsectarian spirit of the rimé movement, which was inaugurated toward the end of the nineteenth century in Kham and had done so much to preserve and invigorate the teachings of all Tibetan schools. Consequently, in addition to his fundamental training in the Nyingma tradition, which included the complete transmission of the teachings of Mipham Rinpoche, Tenpa'i Wangchuk devoted two years to the study of logic and epistemology in the Geluk tradition at the monastery of Amchok Tsenyi in Amdo. And his training was further enriched by the reception of teachings on Prajñāpāramitā and Madhyamaka according to the tradition of the celebrated Jonang master Bamda Thubten Gelek. Furthermore, it is said that inasmuch as Tenpa'i Wangchuk was an incarnation of Yudra Nyingpo and thus directly connected with the yogic power of Guru Rinpoche, when propitious circumstances appeared, his potential as a tertön, or treasure revealer, awakened and he was able to reveal a number of spiritual treasures.

This broadly based training was put to the test, and indeed perfected, in the course of the decades that followed, when, like so many other masters, Tenpa'i Wangchuk had to endure the horrors of the Cultural Revolution and the social changes inflicted by the communist regime. At the age of thirty-one, he was sentenced to twelve years' imprisonment in various gulags. Yet despite these dreadful circumstances, which were intended to be, and might well have proved, the final destruction of Tibet's cultural and spiritual patrimony, the light of the teachings was not extinguished. Indeed, it was during the years of his captivity that Tenpa'i Wangchuk met his most important teachers, prisoners like himself, who, thanks to their previous training of many years, their undimmed faculties, and their great spiritual realization, were able to transmit to him from memory and in situations of great peril, many priceless teachings and pith instructions.

Following his release from imprisonment, and taking advantage of the somewhat more favorable social situation, Tenpa'i Wangchuk single-mindedly devoted the rest of his life to the preservation of the Buddhist teachings. He rebuilt and founded monasteries and places of study where the tradition could be rekindled. He tirelessly guided multitudes of disciples, both Tibetan and Chinese, and composed for them important commentaries and much needed texts of instruction.

In the autumn of 2019, several years after Tenpa'i Wangchuk's death, his nephew and lineage holder, Tsultrim Zangpo Rinpoche, the abbot of Khangsar Taklung Monastery, visited Dordogne in France where he bestowed the full transmission of Tenpa'i Wangchuk's Collected Works, his treasure texts and doctrinal compositions, requesting and thereby inaugurating the present project of translating his published writings into English and subsequently into other Western languages.

The Collected Works

A tireless and skillful teacher, Tenpa'i Wangchuk was also a prolific writer and produced a series of important and fascinating writings, some of which are still being edited. At the moment of writing, the collection comes to eight Tibetan pecha volumes or five Western-style books. In the enormous efforts made to rekindle the Buddhist teachings in Tibet—and to save many teachings that might otherwise have been lost, preserving them for future generations of practitioners both inside and outside Tibet—Tenpa'i Wangchuk committed to writing in clear and accessible form many essential instructions pertaining to both the sūtras and tantras, and most especially to teachings of the Great Perfection. These include expositions of Jigme Lingpa's *Highest Wisdom* (*Ye shes bla ma*) and of Mipham Rinpoche's *Beacon of Certainty* (*Nge shes gron me*). Perhaps most extraordinary of them all are his important and completely unprecedented commentaries on two of Longchenpa's Seven Treasuries: a vast commentary of over 450 pages on *The Precious Treasury of the Dharmadhātu* and a shorter commentary on *The Precious Treasury of the Fundamental Nature*.

Of the five volumes of Tenpa'i Wangchuk's writings currently available, the first begins with Tenpa'i Wangchuk's biography and is followed by a collection of some thirty poems, twenty-six spiritual songs and counsels related to the Great Perfection, and over forty prayers and short practice texts. Many of these are only three or four pages long.

The second volume contains a number of more substantial works related to the sūtra vehicle: a commentary on Gyalse Thogme's celebrated *Thirty-Seven Practices of a Bodhisattva* (*rGyal sras lag len*), autocommentaries on two of Tenpa'i Wangchuk's own poems in the first volume, an instructional text on the four thoughts that turn the mind to the Dharma (*blo ldog rnam bzhi*), and commentaries on three well-known prayers of aspiration—Kunkhyen Jigme Lingpa's *Prayer to Be Reborn in the Copper-Colored Mountain* (*Zangs mdog dpal ri'i smon lam*), Karma Chakme's *Prayer to Be Reborn in Sukhāvatī* (*Chags med bde smon*), and Samantabhadra's *Prayer of Good Action* (*bZang spyod smon lam*).

The remaining three volumes are devoted to several texts related to the Great Perfection. The third volume contains a commentary on *The Cloudless Sky* (*Nam mkha' sprin bral*), a detailed exposition, in the form of a poem, of the practice of *trekchö* by his teacher Togden Lodrö Gyatso; notes on *The Old Yogis' Tradition of Pointing Out the Nature of the Mind* (*Sems ngo mdzub tshugs*) and on Garab Dorje's well-known *Three Lines That Strike the Key Point* (*Tshig gsum gnad brdegs*); an outline of Shabkar Tsokdruk Rangdröl's *Flight of the Garuḍa* (*mKha' lding gshog rlabs*); a word commentary on the inner lama sādhana from Jigme Lingpa's *Heart Essence of the Vast Expanse* (*kLong chen snying thig*), *The Assembly of Vidyādharas* (*Nang sgrub rig 'dzin 'dus pa*); and notes on *Mañjuśrī's Prayer of the Great Perfection* (*'Jam dpal rdzogs pa chen po'i smon lam*).

In the fourth volume we find Tenpa'i Wangchuk's unique commentary on Kunkhyen Longchenpa's *Precious Treasury of the Fundamental Nature* (*gNas lugs rin po che'i mdzod*). This is followed by the text that forms the content of this book—a commentary (*The Light of Wisdom*) on a tantra discovered by the treasure revealer Deshek Lingpa, which is a complete guide to the practice of the Great Perfection titled *The Natural Openness and Freedom of the*

Mind (*Sems nyid rang grol*). Finally, there is a commentary on a pith instruction text of the Great Perfection.

The fifth and final volume is entirely taken up with Tenpa'i Wangchuk's extraordinary commentary on Kunkhyen Longchenpa's *Precious Treasury of the Dharmadhātu* (*Chos dbyings rin po che'i mdzod*).

TRANSLATORS' INTRODUCTION

When, in the eighth century, Guru Padmasambhava entrusted Yeshe Tsogyal with the tantra *The Natural Openness and Freedom of the Mind* and she sealed it within their disciple Yudra Nyingpo's mind, to be extracted as a treasure twelve centuries later by an emanation of Yudra Nyingpo, the treasure revealer Deshek Lingpa,[2] they surely foresaw the growth of interest in the teachings of the Great Perfection currently being shown by students of Tibetan Buddhism, particularly in the West. For this short text contains an unusually complete presentation of the entire path of Dzogchen, clearly explained in his commentary by Deshek Lingpa's spiritual heir, Khangsar Tenpa'i Wangchuk.

Covering the same ground as Jigme Lingpa's famous *Highest Wisdom* and similar texts, it is a practical guide to the whole of the path of the Great Perfection, beginning with the preliminary practices (described in this context as "practices accessory to the view" at the beginning of the main practice), continuing with the two aspects of the main practice, *trekchö* and *thögal*, and ending with a guide to the experiences of the bardo, or intermediate state.

Tenpa'i Wangchuk's commentary on the tantra draws on numerous quotations from other Nyingma masters, in particular Longchenpa, with whose *Precious Treasury of the Fundamental Nature* and *Precious Treasury of the Dharmadhātu* he would, of course, have been thoroughly familiar. It begins in a traditional manner with a brief explanation of its title and the author's homage. It then goes on to describe the setting in which the tantra came into being—not the physical world in which many of the sūtras were taught but the inconceivable dimensions of the various aspects of the three kāyas—and its significance and superiority in relation to other Buddhist teachings. Having thus inspired and prepared the reader for what follows, the text proceeds directly to the main presentation of the practice of the Great Perfection.

Of the two aspects of Dzogchen practice, trekchö and thögal, progress in the latter depends very much on having first gained stability in the practice of the former—that is, the recognition and application of the Dzogchen view. The introduction to this view by a qualified master is typically made once the practitioner has been prepared and is fully receptive to the subtle transmission that is to take place. To facilitate this, therefore, the general principles of the view need to be explained, in particular the distinction between our present deluded state that we call samsara and the completely free state that we call perfect buddhahood or nirvana. Tenpa'i Wangchuk sums this up as follows:

> Within this common [universal] ground there are two aspects: an awareness aspect and an ignorance aspect. The awareness aspect is endowed with the nature, character, and cognizant potency; it is present as a subtle inner luminosity that is gathered within yet not obscured. When it becomes manifest, one is free like Samantabhadra. The ignorance aspect is present like tarnish on gold. When it becomes manifest, one is deluded just as we deluded beings are.

This theoretical basis then has to be reinforced with various practices for purifying the practitioner's body, speech, and mind, beginning with the *rushen* separation practices. These constitute the specific Dzogchen preliminary practices, which, despite their name, should not be confused with the preliminary practices common to all Vajrayāna practices, composed of the five sections of refuge, bodhicitta, confession and purification, offering of the mandala, and guru yoga. Dzogchen cycles such as the Longchen Nyingtik include both these common preliminaries and the specific preliminaries, and the latter do not in any way act as a substitute for the former. Indeed, Dudjom Rinpoche and others have qualified the common preliminaries as even more important than the main practice, and practitioners are unlikely to make any progress in the Great Perfection if their practice is not properly grounded in the preliminaries. Of these, the guru yoga in particular is the very foundation of practice related to the Great Perfection and is considered indispensable each time one begins a session of Dzogchen.

The two parts of the main practice, trekchö and thögal, are traditionally described respectively as the practice without effort for lazy practitioners and the effortful practice for diligent practitioners. These two qualifications are, of course, relative. Serious Dzogchen practitioners aim to attain enlightenment, or at least progress as far as possible, in a single lifetime. Therefore, postponing their practice, engaging in frivolous distractions, and enjoying the pleasures of idleness are hardly likely to form part of their agenda. If trekchö meditation is said to involve nothing to meditate, nothing to do, this is a reference to the absence of the detailed visualizations of the generation phase and the physical exercises of the perfection phase. It does not imply simply lying on one's bed doing nothing, as Milarepa discovered when he sought teachings from the Dzogchen master Rongtön Lhaga but failed to make any progress. On the other hand, the "effort" required for thögal practice is not the strenuous effort needed to perform one hundred thousand full-length prostrations or practice the trulkhor (yogic exercises). It involves, rather, maintaining physical postures and gazes for hours on end without moving and a strict discipline in practicing around the clock.

This division of the practice in terms of two apparently opposed types of individual—lazy and diligent—should not be taken to imply that the two practices are mutually exclusive. While some practitioners will only practice trekchö during their lives, thögal practice cannot be undertaken without having gained a degree of stability in trekchö: Tenpa'i Wangchuk speaks of "the direct path of the union of ground and path—that is, both trekchö as the ground and thögal as the path." Without the foundation of trekchö practice, failure to recognize the visions of thögal as the self-experience of awareness and the consequent dualistic grasping at those visions will prove a fatal hindrance to making progress.

The tantra therefore continues with a detailed account of the nature of awareness, describing what is essentially beyond description by examining its different aspects. Once the view of trekchö has been introduced in this way, it has then to be preserved and stabilized through meditation ("nonmeditation" in this case) and refined through conduct. Tenpa'i Wangchuk summarizes this by quoting Patrul Rinpoche:

> In short, recognizing one's own nature is the view.
> Remaining in that state is the meditation.
> Integrating that with circumstances is the key point of the conduct.
> To make no distinction between view, meditation, and conduct is most important.

The subtle points presented in these sections on the view, meditation, and conduct are by no means easy to understand, and throughout the practice of trekchö, it is all too easy to imagine that one is on the right path when in fact one has fallen victim to errors in one's meditation and deviated from the correct view. In particular, Tenpa'i Wangchuk makes a point of reminding the reader of the dangers of ceasing to respect the karmic law of cause and effect. While the text at this stage provides advice on ensuring that one's meditation is progressing properly, nothing can replace the individual guidance and pith instructions of one's teacher in identifying problems and then remedying them.

Once stable realization of the view of trekchö has been gained, the practice of thögal can be undertaken, as presented in the next section, which introduces the principles of the different postures and gazes, the four or six lamps, and the four visions that are experienced as the practitioner advances on the path. These are followed by a number of pith instructions that enable one to progress. Here again, the text can only provide a sketch that needs to be filled out with personal instructions from the teacher. Other conditions— climatic, geographic, and so on—also need to be taken into account, not to mention a steely determination on the part of the practitioner.

The teaching in this text ends with a brief discussion of the four bardos. For those whose practice of the Great Perfection does not result in buddhahood in their present life, the effects of their practice can still be immensely beneficial at the moment of death and afterward in the bardo of ultimate reality and the bardo of becoming, enabling them to recognize the experiences of these states and to attain liberation then or at least find rebirth in situations in which they can continue to practice and progress spiritually.

In the concluding verses, the treasure revealer Deshek Lingpa mentions the origin and benefits of the tantra, entrusts it to the Dharma protectors, and dedicates it to the enlightenment of all sentient beings.

The Light of Wisdom is followed in Tenpa'i Wangchuk's Collected Works by a short text titled *A Key for Opening the Treasury of Instructions of the Three Lineages*, in which he provides a structural outline (*sa bcad*) of the tantra. In it, each outline heading is listed with the first few syllables of the corresponding section in the root text along with the number of quatrains and/or lines referred to. This presentation is clearly destined for readers who have in their possession a copy of the root text in traditional Tibetan pecha format, without any breaks or other indications between the quatrains of the tantra. Such a presentation is likely to be of little help to Western readers, for whom, in any case, the commentary clearly indicates the relevant sections of the root text. For our translation, therefore, we have attempted to follow the author's original intention of providing a map to help the reader navigate the complexities of the different headings and adapted his text by making use of the numbering and formatting principles that are used in other published translations.

THE GREAT PERFECTION AND SECRECY—A REMINDER TO THE READER

When the translators of this present volume first received instructions on the Great Perfection in the 1970s and 1980s, the teachings were given to a restricted audience, and on a number of occasions those listening were not allowed to record or even write notes during the teachings. Since then, Dzogchen teachings appear to have become more easily accessible, but the fact that books of this kind are now freely available should not tempt readers to think that, complete and detailed though this book is, it can be treated as a sort of "Teach Yourself Dzogchen." The purpose of this text and similar presentations of the Great Perfection is rather to serve as an *aide memoire* for those who have received the corresponding transmissions and the oral instructions that accompany them. All the practices in this book need to be carried out under the constant personal supervision of a qualified master who has true experience of the practice and realization of the Great Perfection. It is important to remember that the transmission of blessing power mediated through a living tradition of realized masters is an indispensable component of the Great Perfection method, without which the introduction to the nature of the mind cannot take place. It should also be noted that the texts of the Great Perfection are invariably placed under the guardianship of powerful spirit protectors, as is the case with the tantra presented in this book (see p. 23), with the result that the misuse of texts and teachings is liable to attract misfortune. Some modern readers may be inclined to dismiss such warnings as folkloric superstition, but it is nevertheless our duty to make them clear and to repeat the traditional admonition that from a self-contrived practice, pursued privately without reference to the tradition, accomplishment is not to be expected.

Acknowledgments

The project to translate the Collected Works into English was initiated by Tsultrim Zangpo Rinpoche, the abbot of Khangsar Taklung Monastery, and Yingrik Drubpa Rinpoche, both disciples of Tenpa'i Wangchuk and trustees of his literary heritage. Having formally asked the Padmakara Translation Group to undertake this ambitious task, they were in turn requested to come to France in the autumn of 2019 so that the translators could receive the necessary empowerments and reading transmissions. It is to them, therefore, that we must first express our profound gratitude for their patience and graciousness in bestowing these. We must then record our thanks to Jigme Khyentse Rinpoche and to Tulku Pema Wangyal Rinpoche who, having accepted Tsultrim Zangpo Rinpoche's request, received him and his entourage in Dordogne and have since unfailingly continued to encourage and inspire the translators in their endeavors. In particular, we acknowledge with immense gratitude the assistance of Khenchen Pema Sherab and Khenpo Sönam Tsewang, both of the monastery of Namdroling in India, in clarifying numerous difficult points. Without their help, this present translation would never have been completed. Finally, thanks are due to Nikko Odiseos, Anna Wolcott Johnson, and the whole team at Shambhala Publications for their support and expertise in seeing this project through to the published book.

This translation was made by Stephen Gethin with the help of Helena Blankleder and Wulstan Fletcher, all of the Padmakara Translation Group. They alone are responsible for any mistakes that have been made, for which they ask the indulgence of the ḍākinīs and protectors of the teachings in accepting their confession.

A Caution for Readers

The practices in this book should only be performed under the personal guidance and supervision of a qualified Dzogchen teacher who is able to ensure that the practitioner has received the appropriate empowerments, transmissions, and practice instructions. Unless the proper conditions have been fulfilled, it is preferable to keep this book respectfully in a safe place until such a time as the necessary authorization to study it has been obtained.

PART ONE

The Natural Openness and Freedom of the Mind

*A Tantra of the Great Perfection from the Mind
Essence of the Lotus Ḍākinī*

DESHEK LINGPA

In Sanskrit: *Mahāsandhyacittasvamuktatantranama*
In Tibetan: *rDzogs pa chen po sems nyid rang grol gyi rgyud ces bya ba*
In English: The Great Perfection Tantra, The Natural Openness and Freedom of the Mind

Homage to the primordial lord!

In the sublime place free of limits and beyond extremes,
The dharmakāya teacher, Samantabhadra,
Teaches the entourage of vidyādharas and ḍākinīs
Who are his own manifestation
The teachings of the resultant secret mantras,
Ineffable and beyond expression,
In the fourth time, the time of primordially pure equality.

This tantra of the ultimate result
Is the life essence of all the lineages of transmission—
The mind transmission of the conquerors
From Samantabhadra, the dharmakāya aspect of the
    dharmakāya,
Through the great Vajrasattva, the dharmakāya aspect of the
    saṃbhogakāya,
To Garab Dorje, the dharmakāya aspect of the nirmāṇakāya;
And the transmissions by symbolic indication and through
    hearing.

It is the essence of the profound key points in the six million
    tantras,
Known as the mind class, space class, and pith instruction class,
Which are intended for beings of basic, moderate, and superior
    faculties.

The profound key points of the buddhas' different teachings—
The Great Middle Way, the Great Seal,
The Great Perfection, and so forth—
Have been combined in this sublime, essential pith instruction.

This is the sole path trodden by all the conquerors—
The track that all the buddhas of the past have left,
The realm in which the buddhas of the present now dwell,
The very goal the buddhas of the future will accomplish.

It will not be realized
Through the philosophical tenet systems of the eight vehicles.
Just as the snow lion's roar subdues the common beasts,
This king of tantras outshines the lesser vehicles.
It is the cause, the way beings attain the result, buddhahood.
There is no other method more ultimate or profound than this—
In a single life and body, one can progress to the vidyādhara
     levels.

The unborn ground expanse,
Naturally arisen and primordially pure,
And the ceaseless display of the appearances of the ground,
Spontaneously present,
Refer to trekchö and thögal—ground and path,
The direct, effortless,
And most profound way of the Great Perfection.

In the beginning, when there is no division into samsara and
     nirvana,
The common ground for freedom as a buddha and delusion as a
     sentient being
Abides as the epitome of the nature, character, and cognizant
     potency,
Present as a subtle inner luminosity, gathered within yet not
     obscured.

When, with the movement of the wisdom wind, awareness rises
    up from the ground,
Tearing the shell of the ever-youthful vase body,
One speaks of "the appearances of the ground manifesting
    through the eight doors of spontaneous presence."
The great vision of samsara and nirvana arises simultaneously—
The appearances of the buddha fields of the three kāyas, without
    limit,
And the boundless realms of one's mind's subjective experience,
Those of the six classes of beings, and so forth.

The instant the appearances of the ground stir,
There is the conviction that they are the self-experience of
    awareness.
As they are recognized as such and particular qualities are
    discerned,
Delusion is purified and primordial wisdom unfolds
As the result ripens within the ground.
Freedom is gained within the ground's primordially pure nature.
This is referred to as Primordial Lord Samantabhadra.

Failing to recognize within the ground the self-experience of
    awareness,
One believes it to be other than it.
The three kinds of ignorance create the cause,
And under the power of the four conditions,
The six kinds of deluded consciousness
Cause the six apprehending cognitive acts to stir unceasingly,
And as a result one is trapped and bound by the six latent
    defilements.
Dualistic clinging to phenomena—
The five aggregates and five senses and their objects—
Is as deceptive as a whirling firebrand,
And the whole variety of appearances
Of the outer container and inner contents manifests.

Through the clinging to a self,
Happiness and suffering are experienced and samsara is produced.
This is just a brief presentation of freedom and delusion.

For someone who, to begin with, is a suitable vessel,
The means for training their mindstream
Are practices that are elaborate, unelaborate,
Extremely unelaborate, or supremely unelaborate,
Depending on the person's disposition and faculties.
For these, the key point is the life-fastening root samaya.

Next, in the rushen separation practice for the three doors,
One's body moves and twists in different ways,
One's speech utters the sounds of the different kinds of beings,
And one's mind imagines all kinds of thoughts,
Both good and bad, uninhibitedly.

Inwardly, in the crown, throat, heart,
Navel, secret center, and soles of the feet of one's body,
Within spheres of light of the six colors,
Are the seeds of the six realms: *a, su, nr,*³ *tri, pre,* and *du.*
In the centers related to the three doors
Are the syllables of the three kāyas of all the buddhas,
A white *oṃ,* red *āḥ,* and blue *hūṃ,*
Each shining with brilliant rays of light.
The fire from them consumes without trace
The seeds and tendencies of the six realms.
For each of these, one hundred thousand recitations are made,
Along with the supplement.

To purify the body, one meditates on a vajra in a blazing mass of
    fire.
To purify the speech, one intones *hūṃ* quietly and forcefully.
To purify the mind, one examines where the mind originates,
    stays, and goes.

One should relax one's three doors in their natural state to render
   them fit.
The key point of the body is to adopt the seven-point posture of
   the path of liberation.
The key point of the speech is to expel the air nine times and
   train in the wind.
The key point of the mind is to develop the motivation of
   compassion for all beings.
One should pray to the teacher, mingle one's mind with the
   teacher's, and receive the four empowerments.

One should examine whether one's body, speech, and mind
Are the same or distinct.
The doer of all things
Is nothing other than the mind.

One should investigate the place from where the mind first comes
And what it is that comes into being;
Examine the place where the mind, in the meantime, dwells
And what it is that dwells;
And look for the place to which, in the end, the mind goes
And what it is that goes.
One should examine in detail whether it has shape or color.
In the same way, one should examine the existence of
   appearances.
When one sees that while appearing,
They are devoid of intrinsic existence,
One should examine whether all that is empty is luminous.
The character of open emptiness is intrinsically luminous.
Since there is no reference point,
One will see unobstructed primordial wisdom.
The mind creates karmic deeds,
And it is the mind that experiences pleasure and pain.
The whole variety of phenomena appear to the mind:
There is nothing that is not created by the mind.

One should closely investigate the nature of the mind
And consider whether seeker and sought are one or two.
One should look for an "I" and the clinging to a self.
When one realizes there is none, one will see that the clinging to
    an "I" is rootless.
One should minutely examine that which sees it:
When one realizes that the seer is certainly groundless, rootless,
One will see the actual condition of things, beyond assertions,
The unborn nature of the path.

The universal ground is the ground
Of the whole of samsara and nirvana;
It is a latent state that remains indeterminate.
It is the ground from which the eight consciousnesses,
The twenty lesser defilements, and other mental factors,
And every single thought proliferate.
The dharmakāya is like clear, unclouded water,
Free of delusion, beyond the realm of the elaborations
Of apprehending subject and apprehended object.
The mind and awareness are like ice and water:
Their nature is the same, but conditions make them different.
The mind is virtuous thoughts—faith and renunciation—
And attachment and aversion to friends and foes, and indifference.

Genuine awareness, the essence that is luminosity,
Sees samsara and nirvana like space, open and unimpeded.
Although, if one elaborates, there are infinite distinctions
Such as the differences between relative and ultimate.
One should examine the difference between realization and lack
    of realization,
Knowledge and ignorance,
To determine what is the fundamental nature.

When one leaves the five sense consciousnesses
In the natural flow without manipulating them,

Without projecting or gathering thoughts, rejecting or accepting,
After the first thought has manifested and disappeared
And in the instant before the next thought arises,
There is awareness of the present moment, fresh and naked.
Its nature, empty from the beginning, is the dharmakāya.
Its character, unobscured, is the saṃbhogakāya.
Its cognizant power, manifesting ceaselessly, is the nirmāṇakāya.

Empty luminosity, luminous emptiness—without any concept of
    it as such,
This alert and wakeful [awareness], untainted by thoughts of the
    past, present, and future,
Is spoken of as "the one and only sphere of the dharmakāya,
    transcending mind."

Genuine awareness, the fourth state in which the other three are
    absent,
Is unobstructed, clear, unobscured, limpid,
A state that is not torpid, that is vivid, unclouded, awake.
Groundless, rootless, it is devoid of birth and cessation.
It does not tend to one side or the other,
And is free from the extremes of permanence and discontinuity,
Unlimited in extent, and beyond coming and going.
It pervades the whole of samsara and nirvana,
Yet it is neither one nor various.
It is free of fixation, without thoughts like "It is this; it is not that."
Though it cannot be indicated by analogy or word,
It is as pure as the sky.
Its own character manifests, openly and unobstructedly.

Ineffable, inconceivable, inexpressible transcendent wisdom,
Unborn, unceasing, with the true nature of space,
Open and free by itself, it is the domain of primordial wisdom
    alone.
Here, there is no ignorance and no awareness.

All the phenomena that appear dualistically as samsara and
   nirvana
Have no existence as perceived objects and perceiving subjects.
From the moment they appear, they are empty by nature;
And while they are empty, by nature they appear.
There is only equality—appearance and emptiness inseparable.
If there is no agent equalizing them as being inseparable,
Neither can there be the act of equalizing in equality.
This primordial wisdom, the luminosity deep within,
Which is beyond the "state of equality,"
Is the dharmakāya, Samantabhadra's wisdom mind.

Potentially either buddha or sentient being,
Mind in its immediate nowness, fresh, unadulterated,
Unobscured, clear and pure in every part—
When one looks at it, one cannot see it;
When one leaves it be, one sees.
From the beginning there has never been
Any deliberate "seeing" of it.

It transcends anything to be attained through meditation.
In this respect, fools fetter themselves:
They talk about accomplishing buddhahood
And look outside and practice energetically.
Although those who practice are [already] buddhas,
They search elsewhere,
And thinking that the buddha cannot be within themselves,
They become depressed.
From the buddha, their own awareness,
They will be cut off for a long time.

When the sun of self-cognizing awareness, the dharmakāya, rises,
The way of abiding, above, of Samantabhadra;
The mode of existence, below, of the hell beings in Torment
   Unsurpassed;

The causes (virtue and evil) and their ripened results, together
    with their root;
The system of the two truths;
Ground, path, and result, and so on;
Subject and object—all these, with nothing mixed,
Are seen with the great primordial wisdom,
Distinctly, as they are.

Though the appearing objects of the six consciousnesses manifest
    unceasingly,
They unfold as the creative power and display of awareness.
The multifarious appearances of samsara and nirvana,
Good and bad, pleasure and pain and their causes,
And subject and object all constitute a single expanse,
A single taste, a single state of evenness.

Appearances are equal, arisings are equal,
Empty phenomena are equal, non-empty phenomena are equal,
Space is equal, everything is equal—
The all-pervading expanse of equality.
Like the reflections in the ocean (which is never changed by
    circumstances)
Of the stars and planets shining in the firmament,
Phenomena manifest clearly and distinctly
In the expanse of the great space [of awareness].
Samsara and nirvana are equal,
Encompassed by the expanse of Samantabhadra.
Sustained calm and profound insight are inseparable,
One taste, the indescribable, inexpressible,
Uncontrived state beyond ordinary mind.
To recognize this nature is the view.

When one encounters the true nature of self-cognizing
    awareness, Samantabhadra,
There is no meditation separate from it.

Through its mere recognition, [thoughts] subside therein.
Apart from that, to fixate on meditation is to obscure the nature
    of awareness.
By resting without looking, one will instantly encounter its true
    nature.
Nonmeditation is the meditation on the natural openness and
    freedom of the mind.

When one has gained stability,
Without any distinction between meditation and
    postmeditation,
Good conduct brings no benefit,
Nor does bad conduct constitute a fault.
Good and bad thoughts, like waves on water,
Subside in four ways in the state of great natural openness and
    freedom;
Like the rays of the sun, they subside by themselves.
This is the conduct that accords
With the natural openness and freedom of the mind.

Whatever meditative experiences, good or bad, occur—
Experiences of bliss, luminosity,
Absence of thought, and so on that one might cling to—
One should not do anything to encourage good ones
Or counteract bad ones;
One should leave them be, free of grasping.
When one settles, free of contrivance and without fixation,
They subside by themselves in the natural state.
The many kinds of deviations, errors, and mistakes can then
    never occur.

As for the twenty-five aspects of the ultimate result that are
    obtained,
The five kāyas are the dharmakāya, saṃbhogakāya, nirmāṇakāya,
Unchanging vajrakāya, and the abhisaṃbodhikāya.

The five kinds of enlightened speech are the ultimate, unborn
    speech;
That which transmits the buddhas' wisdom through symbols;
Expression through words; the inseparable vajra speech;
And the speech of enlightenment, awareness.
The five kinds of enlightened mind are the wisdom of the
    dharmadhātu,
Mirrorlike wisdom, the wisdom of equality,
All-perceiving wisdom, and all-accomplishing wisdom.
The five enlightened qualities are the buddha fields,
Measureless palaces, rays of light, thrones,
And ornaments of enjoyment.
Pacification, increase, gathering under power, wrathful
    subjugation,
And spontaneous deeds are the five enlightened activities.
These aspects of the results are not elsewhere—
They are complete in one's own nature
And truly obtained on the level of Mighty Vajradhara.
This is the teaching on the ground of trekchö,
The stage that combines view and conduct.
It is entrusted to fortunate disciples. Sealed!

The direct path of spontaneous presence, thögal, involving effort,
Is the secret path of luminosity related to the vajra chains:
Through it, hallucinatory appearances (not existing yet appearing
    to exist)
Manifest as the untainted kāyas and wisdoms.
The instructions for manifest buddhahood
Concern the means for attaining it through the four visions—
Called the vision of the dharmatā in reality,
Enhanced experiences of awareness,
The climax of awareness,
And the exhaustion of phenomena transcending ordinary mind.

From the moment it is first formed,
One's body, like a house, is the physical support
In which mind and wisdom are present as what is supported,
Appearing through the pathway of the visual sense organ.
Thanks to the four lamps, all the visions manifest
Like the rays issuing from the sun.
From the natural, original state of calm
There arises the path of profound insight, awareness, the vajra
    chains,
And thence all luminous appearances without exception
    manifest.
Not a single being is there to whom they cannot appear.

First, the nine activities of the three doors must be relinquished.

It is in dependence on four key points that the four lamps appear.
The key point for the body
Refers to the dharmakāya, saṃbhogakāya, and nirmāṇakāya
    postures:
Staying like a lion, elephant, or rishi.
The key point for the sense door is the gaze,
With the eyes turned up, cast down, or looking sideways.
The key point for the speech
Is to train in breathing gently in and out.
The key point for the mind
Is to settle in a state devoid of thoughts of any kind.

The lamp of the empty disks of light,
The lamp of the utterly pure ultimate expanse,
The lamp of self-arisen wisdom,
And that of the far-catching water lasso
Act as cause and result, associated and connected with one another.
The cause is the stage of their vision on the path;
The result is the stage of spontaneous self-manifestation.

How do the four lamps enable the luminous appearances to
   unfold?
The lamp of the empty disks of light
Is the radiance of the lamp of self-arisen wisdom.
The lamp of utter purity and the lamp of the water lasso
Are the conditions for mastering the former two.
The lamp of the expanse provides the space for empty disks,
While the lamp of the far-catching water lasso connects and
   makes them visible.
The lamp of the empty disks acts as the cause for the lamp of self-
   arisen wisdom to manifest;
The lamp of the far-catching water lasso acts as the condition.
The lamp of the pure expanse acts and appears as the ground for
   the manifestation.

In the hollow, blazing jewel of the heart in one's body
Dwells the primordially pure nature of self-arisen primordial
   wisdom,
Empty and unceasingly luminous in character,
Present from the beginning in the guise of a body with face and
   arms.
The means for training in seeing its very appearance in reality
Is what is known as the vajra chains of awareness
Or the lamp of self-arisen wisdom.
Its radiance dwells in the middle of the octagonal palace of the
   heart.

The pure channel known as the crystal kati tube
Has a very fine root and two wide extremities
Like the horns of a gaur, ending in the centers of the eyes.

In the pupils of the eyes—
A half-white, half-black, watery door—
There is the lamp of the far-catching water lasso.

When one looks at the expanse of the sky with half-closed eyes,
Though bluish at first, it later appears very purely,
Unfolding as the five-colored radiance of primordial wisdom,
And the five lights shine like an unfolded brocade.
The radiance of the kāya of the inner expanse
Manifests like reflections in a mirror.

Within the lamp of the utterly pure ultimate expanse,
The self-experience of awareness,
The lamp of the empty disks,
Like ripples from a thrown stone—
Round disks with rims of five-colored light,
And small ones like fish eyes—fleetingly appears.

Inner awareness, extremely limpid, clear, and unceasing,
Manifesting free of limits and beyond extremes—
That is the lamp of self-arisen wisdom.

Within it, there appear the vajra chains of profound insight,
Like golden threads and necklaces of pearls and flowers.
They are the radiance of the lamp of inner awareness shining
     outside.
Holding them captive in the enclosure of the ultimate expanse
     and disks,
One blends the expanse, disks, and awareness into one.
In the beginning, they shake and tremble,
One cannot keep them still for an instant,
And awareness, agitated by the winds, loses control.

The contributory factors for the visions
Are the sun, moon, lamps, crystals, and so forth:
These props are used by day and night
To lead and refine [the rays] from them.
The visions arise from the far-catching lasso alone
Or from all the sense organs.

Focusing on the appearance of the four lamps,
One should concentrate on maturing awareness.
The four lamps are not to be taken separately:
They are like the body and its limbs, like the three kāyas.
By failing to understand the point of the lamp of self-arisen
    wisdom,
Great meditators fixate [on the lamps as different]
And mostly tire themselves out.
Even if they meditate in darkness for a hundred years,
How could that free them from the perilous path of duality?

With the lamp of the far-catching water lasso,
One has the vision of dharmatā in reality.
With the lamp of the empty disks,
One has the vision of the enhanced experiences of awareness.
With the lamp of the utterly pure ultimate expanse,
One has the vision of the climax of awareness.
With the lamp of self-arisen wisdom,
One is brought to the level of the exhaustion of phenomena in
    the dharmatā.

One realizes the four visions
By implementing the key points.
The chains of awareness,
Like scattered knots in horsehair
And clusters of flowers,
Appear indistinctly, shifting and quivering:
Sometimes one sees them, sometimes not.
This is said to be the stage of seeing the dharmatā in reality.

Circular disks of five-colored light,
Straight bands, vertical and horizontal, and so on,
Separate from between the eyes,
And within the expanse of the sky and disks
Appear half bodies of deities and the like.

Deluded perceptions diminish.
This is said to be the stage of the enhanced experiences of
awareness.

In the center of circular disks of five-colored light filling space,
The principal peaceful and wrathful deities and their entourage
all appear.
Samsara and nirvana are realized as the great infinite purity.
All attainments grow to completion like the full moon.
This is said to be the stage of the climax of awareness.

All appearances are gathered into the great sphere.
Like the moon dissolving into space at new moon,
The appearances of phenomena dissolve into the expanse of
dharmatā.
Their exhaustion is not nothingness
But the transfer of appearances toward emptiness.
One has seized the inner luminosity,
The everlasting domain of the youthful vase body.
This is said to be the stage of the great exhaustion of phenomena
beyond mind.

Then there are the supporting instructions called
"Laying the foundation with the three kinds of motionlessness":
The body is kept motionless
So that awareness rests without wavering.
The eyes are kept motionless
So that the ultimate expanse and awareness do not separate.
The winds and awareness are kept motionless
So that luminosity stabilizes and increases.

The extent [of stability] is grasped with the three kinds of
settling:
As appearances settle, the ultimate expanse and awareness will be
free of coming and going.

As the aggregates settle, deluded perceptions will be purified in the
ultimate expanse.
As the wind-mind settles, thoughts will come to exhaustion.

As for grasping the extent of stability in terms of one's dreams:
For those of highest faculties,
Dreams are purified in the ultimate expanse and luminosity
manifests.
Those of middling faculties recognize their nature
And assume and transform different forms in their dreams.
For those of least ability, bad dreams cease.

The signs of proficiency in the four visions
Manifest on the level of body, speech, and mind.

Three signs are associated with the vision of dharmatā in reality:
Physically, one is like a tortoise placed in a metal bowl;
Verbally, one is as if mute, with nothing to say;
And mentally, one stays put, like a bird caught in a trap.

Three signs are associated with the enhanced experiences of
awareness:
Physically, one loses one's self-respect, like someone racked by
illness;
Verbally, one speaks gibberish, like a madman;
And mentally, one is like someone who has been poisoned.

Three signs are associated with the climax of awareness:
Physically, one moves forward like an elephant mired in a swamp;
One's speech is as beautiful as that of a young *kumbhāṇḍa*;[4]
And mentally, one is like someone who has recovered from smallpox.

Three signs are associated with the exhaustion of phenomena in
the dharmatā:
One's body is like a rainbow in the sky;

One's speech repeats what others say, like an echo;
And one's mind is like mist vanishing in the sky.

Because one has attained mastery over outer appearances,
Everything that appears manifests as a buddha field.
Because one has attained mastery over the illusory body on the
    inner level,
One's material body subsides into a pure body of luminosity.
Because one has attained mastery over wind-mind on the secret
    level,
When awareness is directed at the mind of an evil person, that
    person is freed.

Four kinds of immutable great confidence apply the seal:
Confidence free of the hope that one will attain one's goal,
    buddhahood;
And confidence free of the fear that one will not attain it;
Confidence free of the hope that one will cease to wander in
    samsara with its lower realms;
And confidence free of the fear that one will continue wandering.

The ways of gaining freedom
In the four bardos
Are explained in brief.

First is a pith instruction for the natural bardo.
Diligent practitioners with the greatest fortune
Rely on the path of the teacher's profound introduction
And, in meditation and postmeditation,
Mix the experiences of trekchö and thögal with the bardo of
    ultimate reality.
The luminosity of deep sleep being the luminosity of
    dharmakāya,
They train intensely in luminosity during the day
And at night meditate on a five-colored sphere in their heart.

Appearances are meditated on as the nirmāṇakāya buddha field
   of Cāmara
And awareness as Padmasambhava.
This is a profound pith instruction.

Second is the way of gaining freedom in the bardo of the moment
   of death.
In the best case, the three spaces become a single state;
Luminosity, awareness, and emptiness blend inseparably into one.
The two luminosities merge like water into water.
In a single instant, one attains freedom in the primordial ground.
Attaining power over birth, one manifests in the body of great
   transformation;
Attaining power over "entering," one gains freedom in the
   primordial inner ultimate expanse.
Everything is freed in the secret precious dimension.
Those with medium faculties blend consciousness mounted on
   the wind with the dharmadhātu.
Those with basic faculties rely on another person to perform
   transference by joining with *A*.

Third is the way of being freed in the bardo of ultimate reality.
When the consciousness of the universal ground dissolves into
   space,
Primordially pure luminosity appears, clear as the autumn sky;
Having decided that it is nothing other than the display
Of the creative power of awareness in the bardo,
And recognizing it like a child climbing onto its mother's lap,
One attains freedom in the wisdom expanse of Samantabhadra,
Endowed with six special features.
When space dissolves into luminosity,
The appearances of the animate and inanimate world—
The objects outside and what perceives them—subside,
And one's body is seen as light;
Everything that appears manifests as the five lights.

When sounds, lights, rays, and the hosts of wrathful blood-
    drinking deities
And male and female buddhas of the five families, filling space,
Dissolve into one's body, they manifest as the self-experience of
    awareness.
When the state of union dissolves into primordial wisdom,
There manifests the vision of the fourfold primordial wisdom,
The direct path of Vajrasattva—
Fine bands of white, yellow, red, and blue light
Connected with five round lights adorned with five groups of
    disks.
When primordial wisdom dissolves into spontaneous presence,
The appearances of primordial purity manifest
As the eight doors of spontaneous presence:
Awareness manifests as cognizant potency,
And as light, primordial wisdom, deities, nonduality,
Pure freedom from extremes, the door of impurity,
And the door of purity—primordial wisdom.
The display of the creative power of awareness
Dissolves into the ground,
And like an archer's arrow, one is free.

Fourth is the pith instruction on the bardo of becoming.
All fortunate beings who meet with this profound teaching
Will, by the power of truth of the ultimate nature and profound
    interdependence,
As explained above, recognize the self-experience of awareness in
    the bardo.
As if waking from a confused dream,
They will take miraculous birth in the Glorious Mountain of
    Cāmara
Or another nirmāṇakāya buddha field,
And there they will find relief.

This is the ultimate pith instruction: keep it in your heart.

As the entourage of disciples,
[The teacher's] pure self-manifestation, rejoiced,
They were immersed in the unchanging expanse of realization.

The Great Perfection teaching *The Natural Openness and Freedom
    of the Mind*
Is the heart essence of the vidyādhara Garab Dorje,
Which the sublime teacher of mantras Śrīsiṃha taught
To the son of the conquerors, Padmasambhava.
He bestowed it on his wisdom consort, the ḍākinī of Kharchen,
Who, with the aspiration that it should benefit beings of future
    generations,
Sealed it with seven immutable seals
In the precious casket of the expanse of Yudra Nyingpo's mind.

It is the subtle essence of Padmasambhava's mind,
The very heart blood of the hundred thousand ḍākinīs of the
    mother tantras,
The quintessence of omniscient Deshek Lingpa's treasures,
Gathering into one the teachings of the three Heart Essences.
It is extremely profound, the domain of the most fortunate beings.

This profound tantra of the ultimate result
I entrust in whole to the guardians of the Great Perfection teachings—
The sole mother Ekajaṭī, sovereign lady of the mantras,
The yakṣa Shenpa Marnak,
The commander of the eight classes of spirits, and others.
Keep it secret from samaya breakers,
Those with wrong views, unsuitable vessels,
And others who lack fortune, intellectuals and the like.

Someone who says that this does not have the essence of the
    teachings
Will experience the unbearable sufferings of Torment
    Unsurpassed.

All who have faith in this tantra and practice it properly—
The protectors of virtue will constantly in this life watch over
    them.
All living beings without exception
Who see, hear, think of it, or touch it
Will soon attain buddhahood
As the children of the conquerors.
Wherever this teaching is present,
All illnesses and misfortunes will be cleared away;
Long life, good health, and well-being
Will prevail throughout the land.
This tantra is like the wish-fulfilling jewel,
Spontaneously accomplishing the two goals.

At this present time, the very lowest point in the final five
    hundred years,
When the essential teachings are drifting toward Varuṇa the
    water god,
In order to bring fortunate beings of future generations to
    maturity,
I drew this from the casket of the unchanging dharmakāya of my
    mind.

For as long as space endures, may this precious king of tantras
Fully remain for the benefit of infinite sentient beings,
And may they all be completely freed within the precious secret,
The dharmakāya that is doubly pure.

Samaya. Sealed, sealed, sealed.
This completes the text titled *The Great Perfection Tantra, The
Natural Openness and Freedom of the Mind*.

PART TWO

The Light of Wisdom

A Commentary on
The Great Perfection Tantra,
The Natural Openness and Freedom of
the Mind
*from the Mind Essence of
the Lotus Ḍākinī*

KHANGSAR TENPA'I WANGCHUK

namo guru

Samantabhadra, dharmakāya in the buddha field of the
    dharmadhātu,
Buddhas of the five families, saṃbhogakāya endowed with the
    five certainties,
Displays of the nirmāṇakāya in the realms where beings are to be
    trained—
Teachers of the three lineages, manifest within my heart.

Garab Dorje, Mañjuśrīmitra, and Śrīsiṃha,
Jñānasūtra, Padmasambhava, and Vimalamitra,
Omniscient father and son,[5] Deshek Lingpa, and the others,
With unshakable faith, I venerate you a hundred times above my
    head.

That I, a simple-minded man, might explain a little
The key points of the Great Perfection's *Natural Openness and
    Freedom of the Mind*,
A tantra of the most secret and profound fruition aspect,
I beg the permission of the guardians of the teachings and owners
    of the treasure.

The text called *The Great Perfection Tantra, The Natural Openness and Freedom of the Mind* is the quintessence of the six million four hundred thousand tantras of the Great Perfection, bringing together the essential points of the seventeen tantras of the Heart Essence, a profound teaching that appeared as a mind treasure of the great treasure revealer, Deshek Lingpa.[6] It is a pith instruction more precious than the eyes in one's forehead or the blood in one's heart. It is this text, which is like the excellent wish-fulfilling jewel, that I will explain here.

The explanation is divided into three sections: (1) a virtuous beginning, the introduction; (2) a virtuous middle, the text itself; and (3) a virtuous ending, the conclusion. The first of these has two parts: (1) the meaning of the title and (2) the homage.

I. Introduction, the Virtuous Beginning
A. Title

> In Sanskrit: *Mahāsandhyacittasvamuktatantranama*
> In Tibetan: *rDzogs pa chen po sems nyid rang grol gyi rgyud ces bya ba*
> In English: The Great Perfection Tantra, The Natural Openness and Freedom of the Mind

The correspondence between the Sanskrit and Tibetan is as follows. *Mahā* corresponds to *chenpo* (*chen po*), meaning "great." *Sandhya* and its Tibetan equivalent *dzog* (*rdzogs*) mean "perfection." *Citta*, or *semnyi* (*sems nyid*), means "mind (itself)." *Svamukta* corresponds to *rangdröl* (*rang grol*), "natural openness and freedom." *Tantra* is *gyu* (*rgyud*) in Tibetan, meaning "continuum" [but left untranslated as "tantra" in this context]. *Nama*, or *chejawa* (*ces bya ba*) in Tibetan, indicates that the preceding words form a title.

B. Homage

Homage to the primordial lord!

"Primordial lord" refers to the ground awareness free from extremes or the awareness that is the ultimate nature, the object of meditation. It is inseparable from the dharmatā, the nature of all phenomena, or the great dharmadhātu that is the mind of all the buddhas of the three times. In the present context of the path, when the path awareness that has been introduced by one's teacher or the awareness that is cognizant power, the meditating subject, arrives at the awareness that is the ultimate nature, the object of meditation, the ground awareness and path awareness blend inseparably into one taste. It is to these ground and path awarenesses, inseparable as a single flavor, that homage (of the best kind)[7] is paid by meeting with the view.

II. The Text Itself, the Virtuous Middle

The text itself is divided into (1) preliminaries, (2) main practice, and (3) conclusion.[8] The first of these has five parts: (1) a description of the setting for this tantra; (2) the manner in which the key points of the infinite tantras are included within this tantra; (3) showing that this tantra is the essence of all the different teachings of the buddhas; (4) showing that it is the sole path trodden by the buddhas past, present, and future; and (5) showing how it outshines all the intellectual philosophical tenet systems of the eight vehicles. The first of these, the setting, is divided into a brief outline and a detailed explanation.

A. Preliminaries
1. The Setting
a. Brief Outline

> In the sublime place free of limits and beyond
>   extremes,
> The dharmakāya teacher, Samantabhadra,
> Teaches the entourage of vidyādharas and ḍākinīs
> Who are his own manifestation
> The teachings of the resultant secret mantras,
> Ineffable and beyond expression,
> In the fourth time, the time of primordially pure
>   equality.

The setting for this tantra is as follows. The perfect location is the sublime place that is the unexcelled dharmadhātu, which is free of limits and beyond extremes—it is not in any way delimited, neither does it fall into any extremes. In that place there dwells the perfect teacher, the dharmakāya teacher Samantabhadra, teaching the perfect retinue, an inconceivable entourage of vidyādharas and ḍākas and ḍākinīs who manifest unceasingly as the self-display of awareness, which is no different from him. The perfect teaching is the most secret resultant teaching of Ati, the quintessence of the three inner tantras of the Secret Mantrayāna. No words can describe it; it cannot be voiced or imagined. The perfect time is the nonconceptual time of primordially pure equality, the timeless fourth time transcending past, present, and future. It is with these five perfections that the tantra was taught.

b. Detailed Explanation

> This tantra of the ultimate result
> Is the life essence of all the lineages of
> transmission—
> The mind transmission of the conquerors
> From Samantabhadra, the dharmakāya aspect of the
> dharmakāya,
> Through the great Vajrasattva, the dharmakāya
> aspect of the saṃbhogakāya,
> To Garab Dorje, the dharmakāya aspect of the
> nirmāṇakāya;[9]
> And the transmissions by symbolic indication and
> through hearing.

This tantra is a tantra of the resultant doctrine, the Vajrayāna, which is superior to the eight graded vehicles. It is the highest of all the sacred teachings.

The perfect place for this is the realm of the dharmakāya, the buddha field in which the three kāyas of all the buddhas manifest. It is the place in which the ultimate expanse and primordial wisdom are of one taste, called Akaniṣṭha (The Unexcelled). It is entirely devoid of the conceptual elaborations concerning above and below, periphery or center. It is called The Unexcelled because it is above all phenomena and there is no other phenomenon higher than it. However, this is not the same as The Unexcelled that is the realm in which our teacher Samantabhadra Vajradhara taught the tantras.

It is within such a perfect place, The Unexcelled, that the perfect teacher, Samantabhadra, the dharmakāya aspect of the dharmakāya, beyond all conceptual construction, ["teaches"] his perfect entourage, which is no different from him. The perfect time is that of the utterly immutable ultimate reality. And the perfect teaching is this tantra, *The Natural Openness and Freedom of the Mind* (the mind's nature, which never stirs from concentration), which arises in the continuum of his mind without any conceptual constructs in the form of words. This is mentioned in a tantra:

> The tathāgata communicates in a special way with the tathāgatas.[10]

This is the ground for the unfolding of the tantra.

Similarly, in the context of the saṃbhogakāya aspect of the dharmakāya, the perfect teacher is the saṃbhogakāya, emptiness and luminosity inseparable. The place is the uncontaminated state free of obscuration. The time is that of ultimate reality, beyond permanence or discontinuity. The teaching is that of the ineffable meaning. And the entourage is the teacher's own empty exclusive self-experience.

Again, in the context of the nirmāṇakāya aspect of the dharmakāya, the teacher is the unimpeded ground for the arising of the nirmāṇakāya aspect of the dharmakāya. The place is present as the ground of arising that does not exist in any way. The teaching is that of meditative concentration, unceasing and luminous. The entourage is the three kāyas present in the state of awareness. The time is that of the manifestation of the fundamental nature, the quintessence. These are not the usual authentic perfections: they are conceptual ascriptions for distinguishing five aspects in a single emptiness. Thus, the teacher and entourage, which transcend the details of faces and attributes, refer to the great all-pervading equality of the ultimate expanse and primordial wisdom.

These explanations of the dharmakāya must be understood as referring only to the ceaseless radiance of the inner luminosity that is able to manifest as the display of the outwardly radiating luminosity. They should not be understood as referring to the outwardly radiating luminosity itself.

Thus, in the context of the dharmakāya, the nature, character, and cognizant potency or the dharmakāya, saṃbhogakāya, and nirmāṇakāya, along with the five perfections, need to be distinguished on the basis of a single empty nature, as is stated in *Self-Illuminating Awareness*:

> Unchanging, unimpeded, all-pervading—
> These three are the nature of the dharmakāya.

If you wish to go into this in greater detail, you should study Longchenpa's Seven Treasuries. In brief, the manner in which the lineages of the dharmakāya, saṃbhogakāya, and nirmāṇakāya aspects are explained in the context of the dharmakāya is as follows. Since they are no different from the aspects of a single primordially pure awareness, the wisdom minds of all the conquerors extend evenly as a single taste in the expanse of the actual primordial wisdom of ultimate reality that does not exist in any way outside or inside, above or below, or of the great primordial wisdom that abides in the ground of the dharmakāya; and this is what we call "the mind lineage of the conquerors."

In a similar vein, where the root verse says "Vajrasattva, the dharmakāya aspect of the saṃbhogakāya," I think it is implying that Vajrasattva is the sovereign embodiment of all the hundreds of buddha families. Apart from that, in the context of the dharmakāya aspect of the saṃbhogakāya, the perfect place is the buddha field of the Dense Array. The teacher is the buddha Vairocana Mahāsāgara, whose entourage is no different from him. The teaching is that of the self-arisen primordial wisdom, his own self-experience. The time is that of the manifestation of realization.

Again, in the context of the saṃbhogakāya aspect of the saṃbhogakāya, the teacher is the lord of the family of whichever tantra is being expounded. The place is the Dense Array, the entourage is the assembly of deities of each of the five families, the teaching is that of the five kinds of primordial wisdom, and the time is that of the gathering in and spreading out of light.

In the context of the nirmāṇakāya aspect of the saṃbhogakāya, the teacher is any one of the buddhas of the five families. The entourage comprises the inconceivable hundreds of thousands of male and female deities enjoying the self-experience of awareness. The place is the completely uncompounded Willow Leaf realm. The Willow Leaf realm in this case is said to be the realm of each of the five buddha families: it is not referring to the buddha field of Vajrapāṇi. The time is the time of the self-experience of awareness.

To sum up, it is taught that in the context of the saṃbhogakāya, one speaks of the saṃbhogakāya's exclusive self-experience; it is important to be clear that it has nothing to do with what is perceived by other beings. As we read in *The Precious Treasury of the Dharmadhātu*,

> The saṃbhogakāya nature
> Is a character [of luminosity]
> Spontaneously present.
> Its display consists of the five families
> And the five primal wisdoms,
> Which appear and fill the whole of the expanse of space.[11]

Now, for "Garab Dorje, the dharmakāya aspect of the nirmāṇakāya," in the context of the dharmakāya aspect of the nirmāṇakāya, the teacher is Garab Dorje manifesting in the form of Vajradhara. The place is the realm of the thousand lotuses. The entourage comprises beings who take the four kinds of birth. The teaching is the *Word-Transcending Root Tantra*, which is the root of all the scriptural collections. The time is the time when beings' lives last an infinite number of years.

In the context of the saṃbhogakāya aspect of the nirmāṇakāya, the teacher is Vajrasattva, the place is a billion billionfold universes, the entourage consists of bodhisattvas on the eighth level, the teaching is that of the vehicle of the definitive meaning, and the time is not fixed.

In the context of the nirmāṇakāya aspect of the nirmāṇakāya, the teacher is Śākyamuni, the place is a billion Sahā worlds with their four continents, the entourage consists of celestial beings, humans, and the like, the teaching is that of the causal and resultant vehicles, and the time is the definite time for the clearing away of doubts. With regard to this, *The Precious Treasury of the Dharmadhātu* states,

> The nature of nirmāṇakāya is cognizant potency,
> Which is the ground of arising.
> Its display appears according to the needs
> Of beings to be guided
> And has mastery of great enlightened action.[12]

The nirmāṇakāya is endowed with enlightened body, speech, mind, qualities, and activities. Its body has all the major and minor marks. Its speech possesses the sixty tones of Brahmā. Its mind knows all that is to be known. It has all the excellent qualities complete. And its activities are applied on a vast scale to benefit beings.

These explanations are based on Omniscient Longchenpa's Seven Treasuries.

To sum up, this text, *The Great Perfection Tantra, The Natural Openness and Freedom of the Mind,* was transmitted from the dharmakāya aspect of the dharmakāya Samantabhadra to the dharmakāya aspect of the saṃbhogakāya Vajrasattva, who in turn transmitted it to the dharmakāya aspect of the nirmāṇakāya Garab Dorje. Since the wisdom minds of the conquerors are of a single taste in the dharmadhātu, this constitutes the conquerors' lineage of mind transmission. Then, teachers who appear as humans and nonhumans transmit all the teachings of the mind transmission lineage by means of symbols, and this constitutes the vidyādharas' lineage of transmission by symbolic indication. Again, all the teachings of the mind and symbol lineages are transmitted from one individual to another through the lineage of transmission by hearing. This tantra is thus the secret quintessence of the instructions of the entire mind, symbol, and hearing transmissions, like the vital essence of life, the heart's elixir, which, in terms of its perfect setting, is taught as being especially sublime.

2. The Manner in Which the Key Points of the Infinite Tantras Are Included within This Tantra

> It is the essence of the profound key points in the six
>   million tantras,
> Known as the mind class, space class, and pith
>   instruction class,
> Which are intended for beings of basic, moderate,
>   and superior faculties.

The great master Garab Dorje went miraculously to the buddha field of Manifest Joy in the east and received from the buddha Vajrasattva an inconceivable number of tantras of the Great Perfection. He compiled all their teachings in six million four hundred thousand tantras and entrusted them to Mañjuśrīmitra. All the profound points in those tantras are included here in this single [tantra]. It is thus the quintessence of their intended meaning, just as butter is the essence of churned milk. The master Mañjuśrīmitra compiled these six million four hundred thousand tantras of the Great Perfection into three classes, known as the outer mind class, inner space class, and secret pith instruction class, intending them for three kinds of beings. For beings of basic faculties who are inclined to mind,[13] there are the so-called mind class teachings; for those of moderate faculties inclined to space, there is the space class; and for those with the best or highest faculties, who do not need to make the efforts required on the graded path, there is the secret pith instruction class. All these teachings are included here in this tantra. Furthermore, Śrīsiṃha divided the secret pith instruction class into four major cycles, as has been said:

> The outer cycle is like the body, extensively teaching in
> words.
> The inner cycle is like the eyes: visual teachings with
> symbols.
> The secret cycle is like the heart: teachings for unforgetting
> memory.
> And this [unsurpassed, most secret cycle] is like a person
> whose body is whole and complete.

Thus, all the profound key points of the most secret pith instructions are included in this tantra.

3. Showing That This Tantra Is the Essence of All the Different Teachings of the Buddhas

> The profound key points of the buddhas' different
> teachings—
> The Great Middle Way, the Great Seal,
> The Great Perfection, and so forth—
> Have been combined in this sublime, essential pith
> instruction.

According to the Sūtra Vehicle of Transcendent Perfections, there are eighty-four thousand collections of teachings that were given to remedy the eighty-four thousand different defilements. Of these and others of the buddhas' inconceivably numerous ways of teaching, the highest is the Great Middle Way (Madhyamaka) in which the ground middle way is the union of the two truths, the path middle way is the union of the two accumulations, and the resultant middle way is the union of the two kāyas. The ultimate meaning of these is included here in this tantra.

Furthermore, there is the Luminous Great Seal (Mahāmudrā), the way of nonmeditation, which is practiced in eighteen lineages, including the four major and eight minor schools of the Kagyu tradition, which came down from Tilopa, Naropa, and other great siddhas in the noble land of India and through Marpa, Milarepa, Dagpo Gampopa, and other sublime accomplished beings in the Land of Snows. The key points of this tradition too are included here.

And this very tantra is a sublime, quintessential pith instruction that condenses the profound key points of the pith instructions of the kama and terma lineages of the Luminous Great Perfection, which was the principal practice of the great accomplished beings of the Nyingma tradition of the Secret Mantrayāna. These include the great vidyādharas of India—Garab Dorje, Mañjuśrīmitra, Śrīsiṃha, Padmasambhava, and Vimalamitra—and, in Tibet, the twenty-five disciples (the king and subjects) and other accomplished beings.

4. Showing That This Tantra Is the Sole Path Trodden by the Buddhas Past, Present, and Future

> This is the sole path trodden by all the conquerors—
> The track that all the buddhas of the past have left,
> The realm in which the buddhas of the present now dwell,
> The very goal the buddhas of the future will
> accomplish.

The sole, sublime path that all the conquerors tread to the level of the ultimate result is this very tantra. In what way? In the past, Buddha Dīpaṃkara and countless other buddhas who have come all attained freedom by relying on this natural, effortless path of the Great Perfection. So it is the track that the buddhas of the past have left. Similarly, Buddha Śākyamuni and other buddhas of the present era also attained freedom by realizing this great equality, the dharmadhātu beyond elaborations, so it is the realm in which the buddhas of the present now dwell. And for the nine hundred and ninety-six buddhas of the future too, headed by Lord Maitreya, it will be impossible to attain freedom without relying on this path. Therefore, this tantra comprises the very goal that the buddhas of the future will accomplish.

5. Showing How This Tantra Outshines All the Intellectual Philosophical Tenet Systems of the Eight Vehicles

> It will not be realized
> Through the philosophical tenet systems of the
>   eight vehicles.
> Just as the snow lion's roar subdues the common beasts,
> This king of tantras outshines the lesser vehicles.
> It is the cause, the way beings attain the result,
>   buddhahood.
> There is no other method more ultimate or profound
>   than this—
> In a single life and body, one can progress to the
>   vidyādhara levels.

With the philosophical tenet systems of the eight vehicles—from the Listeners' Vehicle, which is the lowest of the three general vehicles that lead one away from the origin of suffering, to the Vehicle of Anuyoga, which is one of the three vehicles of mastery by secret means—one will never realize the topics that are taught in the profound teachings of the most secret, unsurpassable Atiyoga. As Longchenpa says,

> From the summit of the king of mountains,
> Once it has been scaled,
> The valleys down below can all be seen at once,

But from these valleys down below the peak cannot be seen.
Likewise, the vajra essence of the Atiyoga,
The highest peak of all the vehicles
Surveys the goals of all these vehicles
But is to them invisible.[14]

This Vehicle of Atiyoga can be likened to the snow lion, the "five-headed lord," whose roar completely subdues ordinary beasts such as foxes and monkeys. In the same way, all the inferior views of the lower vehicles are completely overshadowed by the spontaneous thunder of this king of tantras, the very pinnacle of all vehicles, in which are taught such topics as the limitlessness of space pervading all the phenomena of samsara and nirvana, the great groundless, rootless state, the objectless, open and unimpeded display, the great primordial wisdom that pervades the whole of samsara and nirvana.

In this regard, the cause of our attaining buddhahood in the future is the ultimate, uncontrived primordial wisdom that is present from the very beginning in the minds of all ordinary sentient beings—or the innate primordial wisdom that has never separated from us from the very beginning; and it is this that is awakened by the sublime teacher's pith instructions. By practicing the path, one accomplishes the primordial wisdom of the four visions of spontaneous presence, and in this life, phenomenal appearances are exhausted in the expanse of ultimate reality. One attains the result, buddhahood, as the primordial lord, the all-pervading sovereign and epitome of the four kāyas and five kinds of primordial wisdom. There is not a single pith instruction that is more profound or ultimate than this marvelous method for attaining buddhahood. In what way? Because in a single life, in a single body, one can progress without difficulty to the four vidyādhara levels.

B. Main Practice

The explanation of the main practice is divided in (1) a brief outline and (2) a detailed explanation.

1. Brief Outline

> The unborn ground expanse,
> Naturally arisen and primordially pure,
> And the ceaseless display of the appearances of the
>   ground,
> Spontaneously present,
> Refer to trekchö and thögal—ground and path,
> The direct, effortless,
> And most profound way of the Great Perfection.

What we call the way of trekchö is that which emphasizes the awareness of the unborn, self-arisen, primordially pure ground expanse. And what we call the way of thögal, spontaneous presence, is that which emphasizes the appearances of the kāyas and wisdoms, the ceaseless display of the appearances of the ground that manifest spontaneously. By relying on the direct path of the union of ground and path—that is, both trekchö as the ground and thögal as the path—in this life one will actualize the primordial wisdom of the four visions of spontaneous presence and one will conquer the level of the primordial buddha, Samantabhadra. This is the way of the Great Perfection, effortless and most profound.

This was a brief introduction to what follows.

2. Detailed Explanation

The detailed explanation has two main sections: (1) the practice of primordial purity, trekchö—the path by which lazy persons gain freedom without effort; and (2) the practice of spontaneous presence, thögal—by which diligent persons gain freedom through effort. The first of these is divided into four parts, of which the first, establishing the view of the ground, is further divided into two, beginning with a general description of the practices accessory to the view. This is again divided into nine parts, of which the first, an explanation of the distinction between samsara and nirvana, freedom and delusion, is presented under four headings, beginning with a presentation of the original common ground.[15]

a. The Practice of Primordial Purity, Trekchö—the Path by Which Lazy Persons Gain Freedom without Effort
i. Establishing the View of the Ground
A) A General Description of the Practices Accessory to the View
1) An Explanation of the Distinction between Samsara and Nirvana, Freedom and Delusion
a) A Presentation of the Original Common Ground

> In the beginning, when there is no division into
> samsara and nirvana,
> The common ground for freedom as a buddha and
> delusion as a sentient being
> Abides as the epitome of the nature, character, and
> cognizant potency,
> Present as a subtle inner luminosity, gathered
> within yet not obscured.

In the very earliest beginning, there was no division into samsara and nirvana, or, in other words, there were not even the names "samsara" and "nirvana." It was before a single buddha attained buddhahood, a time when not a single being was deluded. At that time, there was nothing apart from the original common ground, like space, in which there is no top and bottom, no center and periphery, no directions and intermediate directions, as is stated in the *Tantra of Samantabhadra*:

> The universal ground is uncompounded,
> An all-pervading vast expanse that nothing can express.
> If one knows it, one is buddha;
> If one fails to recognize it, one is deluded and wanders in
> samsara.

This original common ground is not by nature either freedom or delusion, and so it is spoken of as a third kind of ground, or as an indeterminate state. Thus it is said in the *Tantra of the Expanse of Samantabhadra's Wisdom*,

> The universal ground is the common ground of all samsara and nirvana.
> It is like the sleeping state when one's senses are unaware of their objects.
> In the five states in which the mind is not manifest, it is present as a latent condition of the nature of the mind and the ordinary mind (the support and the supported).[16]

The manner in which this universal ground is the common ground of both freedom and delusion is mentioned in the *Tantra of the Expanse of Samantabhadra's Wisdom*:

> The common ground of everything, samsara and nirvana.

And the *Stainless Tantra of Mañjuśrī* says,

> The universal ground is the common ground of everything,
> The ground of samsara and nirvana
> And of complete purity.

And in the *Tantra of the Expanse of Samantabhadra's Wisdom* we read,

> It is not sentient beings, or buddhas, or the primordial wisdom of the path, or the nature of the mind. Since it is the container for everything or the ground for their arising, it is called the "universal ground."

Within this common ground there are two aspects: an awareness aspect and an ignorance aspect. The awareness aspect is endowed with the nature, character, and cognizant potency; it is present as a subtle inner luminosity that is gathered within yet not obscured.[17] When it becomes manifest, one is free like Samantabhadra. The ignorance aspect is present like tarnish on gold. When it becomes manifest, one is deluded just as we deluded beings are.

b) How the Appearances of Spontaneous Presence Unfold

> When, with the movement of the wisdom wind,
>   awareness rises up from the ground,
> Tearing the shell of the ever-youthful vase body,
> One speaks of "the appearances of the ground
>   manifesting through the eight doors of
>   spontaneous presence."
> The great vision of samsara and nirvana arises
>   simultaneously—
> The appearances of the buddha fields of the three
>   kāyas, without limit,
> And the boundless realms of one's mind's subjective
>   experience,
> Those of the six classes of beings, and so forth.

Within the expanse of the original common ground, the wisdom wind stirs in the form of a web of five-colored light. This creates the ground for the manifestation, which gives rise to the appearances of the five-colored lights of spontaneous presence. At that time, awareness rises up from the ground, tearing the shell of the ever-youthful vase body. As this happens, just as when sunlight strikes a crystal it shines with five-colored light, we speak of "the appearances of the ground manifesting through the eight doors of spontaneous presence,"[18] and the appearances of the buddha fields of the three kāyas and so on, without limit, arise. If, at that moment, one recognizes them as the self-experience of awareness, one is free; but if one fails to recognize them as such, one is obscured by coemergent ignorance, like the breaking of the day at dawn being obscured by clouds. Subsequently, conceptual ignorance grows: the boundless impure realms of the mind's subjective experience, those of the six classes of beings, and so on, proliferate, and one is deluded by considering one's own mind's subjective experience to be something other.

Where the root verse says, "The great vision of samsara and nirvana arises simultaneously," it is simply referring to the fact that there is a single ground for the arising of both the appearances of nirvana (if there is recognition) and the appearances of samsaric existence (where there is no recognition). "Samsara" and "nirvana" have never existed as two separate things, and it is with this in mind that it speaks of "arising simultaneously." But from the point of view of the individual, the way of arising is not simultaneous: it occurs at different times.

c) How, When One Recognizes One's Own Nature, One Is Freed Directly within the Primordial Ground

> The instant the appearances of the ground stir,
> There is the conviction that they are the self-
>   experience of awareness.
> As they are recognized as such and particular
>   qualities are discerned,
> Delusion is purified and primordial wisdom unfolds
> As the result ripens within the ground.
> Freedom is gained within the ground's primordially
>   pure nature.
> This is referred to as Primordial Lord
>   Samantabhadra.

When the appearances of the ground—that is, appearances of spontaneous presence— manifest, in the first instant, the dharmakāya Samantabhadra stirs or knows them and is aware of them. In the second instant, he has the certainty that the five lights are the self-experience of awareness: he recognizes the appearances of the ground as his own self-experience,[19] discerns its particular qualities, and so on. In short, he is endowed with the six special features [of Samantabhadra]: [appearances of the ground are] superior to the ground; they are the self-experience of awareness; the particular qualities [of the ultimate expanse] are discerned; freedom occurs on the basis of this discernment; freedom does not arise through the intervention of extraneous factors; and it dwells in its own place. In the third instant, delusion is purified in its own place, and all the qualities of primordial wisdom unfold naturally as the twenty-five qualities of the result ripen within the ground. The fundamental nature, the primordially pure nature, is realized, and all the appearances of outwardly radiating luminosity—the kāyas and primordial wisdoms—dissolve into inner luminosity, the subtle primordial wisdom that is gathered within but not obscured. Freedom is gained within the ground, and the two goals are perfected. This is buddhahood, referred to as Primordial Lord Dharmakāya Samantabhadra.

Thus, Samantabhadra is free and has never been deluded. Ordinary, deluded beings like us are deluded and have never been free. If one has experienced both delusion and freedom, one is like our teacher, Śākyamuni. And the state that is neither free nor deluded is that of dwelling in the expanse of the original common ground, neither free nor deluded.

d) How, When One Fails to Recognize One's Own Nature, One Is Deluded and Thus Wanders in Samsara

> Failing to recognize within the ground the self-
> experience of awareness,
> One believes it to be other than it.
> The three kinds of ignorance create the cause,
> And under the power of the four conditions,
> The six kinds of deluded consciousness
> Cause the six apprehending cognitive acts to stir
> unceasingly,

> And as a result one is trapped and bound by the six
>   latent defilements.
> Dualistic clinging to phenomena—
> The five aggregates and five senses and their objects—
> Is as deceptive as a whirling firebrand,
> And the whole variety of appearances
> Of the outer container and inner contents
>   manifests.
> Through the clinging to a self,
> Happiness and suffering are experienced and
>   samsara is produced.
> This is just a brief presentation of freedom and
>   delusion.

Even though there is no delusion in the ground, one may fail to recognize within the ground all the manifestations of the precious spontaneous presence (that is, the ground appearances) as the self-experience of awareness and believe them to be other than it. How does this happen? For example, ultimate reality becomes the ground of delusion for the object, the five lights become the ground of delusion for the container [and contents], and awareness becomes the ground of delusion for the mind—thus one is deluded.

To say a little bit more on how this happens, when one fails to recognize ultimate reality—primordially pure emptiness, perfectly pure from the very beginning—and one thinks, "What is this empty nothing?" it becomes the ground of delusion for the object. As for the five lights becoming the ground of delusion for the container and contents, when the five lights appear as if sunlight had fallen on the clear crystal of the inseparability of ultimate nature and character, one may grasp at them dualistically and think, "Have the lights over there come from me, or have I come from the five lights?" and they thus become the ground of delusion for the container and contents. With regard to awareness becoming the ground of delusion for the mind, although there is no impure delusion in self-arisen awareness, it may be adulterated by the contaminants of ignorance, dualistic apprehension, and wind-mind, and thus it becomes the ground of delusion of sentient beings.

At that time, "the three kinds of ignorance create the cause." When the five lights manifest as outwardly radiating luminosity, in failing to recognize them as the self-experience of awareness, one is obscured by the universal ground as if by deep sleep. That universal ground exists as ignorance concomitant with cognition, and when it is not aroused toward an object, it is ignorance as the cause [of the other two kinds of ignorance], the ignorance that has the same nature [as awareness].

When it is slightly aroused toward an object, it fails to recognize appearances as awareness's own radiance, resulting in a hazy cognition devoid of mindfulness, which is coemergent ignorance. These two kinds of ignorance are respectively subtle and more gross.

Finally, based on the perpetuation of each of these, there is conceptual ignorance, or the defiled consciousness. In this way the three kinds of ignorance create the cause [of delusion]. One then falls under the power of four conditions. This is explained by Omniscient Jigme Lingpa as follows:

> The causal condition is the ground itself
> Abiding like a dwelling place.
> When perception and discernment arise therein, this is the
>   dominant condition.
> Thence arise the object and the subject, the objective
>   condition.
> And these three coinciding form the immediately preceding
>   condition.[20]

These four conditions are:

- the causal condition, the ground itself manifesting as the five lights,
- the dominant condition, which is the aspect of the discerning cognition,

· the objective condition, which makes a distinction between object and subject, and
· the immediately preceding condition, which is the adventitious proliferation of the appearances of samsara when these three conditions occur simultaneously.

There is also a presentation according to which the three kinds of ignorance, as mentioned above, are the cause and the immediately preceding condition is the three causes and four conditions.

Thus, under the influence of obscuring ignorance, the emptiness-clarity aspect, which pervades equally the ground and the mind, creates the cause, while the display of the movements of the karmic wind creates the conditions. In this way, through the interdependence of cause and conditions coinciding, all the appearances that are the objects of the six consciousnesses—forms, sounds, smells, tastes, physical sensations, happiness, suffering, and so forth—proliferate, and based on that, the six kinds of cognitive act that apprehend each of those objects stir unceasingly; and from this come the six latent defilements. Like the red flames that flicker when the bellows are directed onto a fire hidden under the ashes, the six defilements increase and, on that basis, one is trapped and bound by the six defilements. As a result of the clinging to a self in the five aggregates internally and the five sense objects externally, and so on—in short, in the appearances of the oceanlike realm of phenomena—apprehending subject and apprehended object are considered to be two things, and deluded beings are deceived by them as if by whirling firebrands. The various appearances of the container and contents—the vast vessel that is the world outside, the innumerable sentient beings that are the contents inside it, and the unstable, beautiful array of the pleasures of the five senses and so forth in between—all these manifest, grasped at as if they existed even though they do not.

In this way, grasping at the objects that appear as having a self constitutes the cause of delusion, and discursive thoughts constitute the conditions, and when they come together interdependently,

THE LIGHT OF WISDOM — 49

the deluded perceptions of the three worlds—experiences of happiness, suffering, indifference, and so on—unfold indefinitely and produce what we call "samsara."

Thus, if all the appearances of spontaneous presence—that is, the ground appearances within the ground—are recognized as the self-experience of awareness, there is freedom. And if they are not recognized, there is delusion. All this was just a brief presentation of freedom and delusion.

2) Showing How It Is Necessary to Train in Whichever of the Four Yogas Is Appropriate, Depending on the Dispositions and Faculties of the Disciples

> For someone who, to begin with, is a suitable vessel,
> The means for training their mindstream
> Are practices that are elaborate, unelaborate,
> Extremely unelaborate, or supremely unelaborate,
> Depending on the person's disposition and faculties.
> For these, the key point is the life-fastening root
> samaya.

To begin with, it is necessary to check whether or not the disciple is a suitable vessel for the Great Perfection. The means by which a disciple who is a suitable vessel trains their mindstream are as follows. In general, individuals who are suitable vessels for practicing the Great Perfection are of three kinds: instantaneous practitioners who gain realization at a single stroke, gradual practitioners who progress in stages, and practitioners who skip stages. Of these, the instantaneous practitioners are further divided into instantaneous-instantaneous, gradual-instantaneous, and skipper-instantaneous practitioners, and the gradual and skipper practitioners are similarly divided into three kinds, making nine classes in all. All these can be regrouped according to four kinds of practice: elaborate, unelaborate, extremely unelaborate, and supremely unelaborate, each of which accords with the particular disposition and faculties of the practitioner, for whom the key point is the root samaya that binds the life of the practice. There are numerous instructions on this.

If we then regroup these different classes of practitioner, they can be condensed into two: those who perceive everything as the self-experience of awareness and those who perceive what they see as sense objects. In the first case, the teacher is a practitioner with the highest realization, and the disciple is someone with faith and pure samaya, for whom the enduring karma of aspirations made in previous lives has awakened and the time is now right. In such a case, when teacher and disciple meet, there is no need for the disciple to prepare by analyzing the nature of the mind: he or she is given the introduction directly. In the best case, there occurs "the coming together of three authentic signs": as soon as the introduction is made, it is said, "all phenomena manifest as ultimate reality, appearances and mind mingle inseparably, and view and meditation are instantaneous." Examples of such disciples include the vidyādhara Garab Dorje and the beggar Mipham Gönpo. However, in less fortunate cases, there is a danger of the view of emptiness becoming a vast blank—Hashang's view—and turning into a kind of thoughtless sustained calm, so the risks are as extreme as the possible benefits. For this reason, for practitioners who perceive what they see as sense objects, there is the way of preliminary analysis, whereby the practitioner begins by destroying the inner sanctum of the mind, investigating the mind, seeking out the mind's weak point, and so on. This way is free of hindrances and deviations.

3) The Outer Rushen Separation Practice for the Three Doors

> Next, in the rushen separation practice for the three
>   doors,
> One's body moves and twists in different ways,
> One's speech utters the sounds of the different kinds
>   of beings,

And one's mind imagines all kinds of thoughts,
Both good and bad, uninhibitedly.

Next, we shall explain the separation practice for the three doors.[21] As it is said in the *Only Child of the Teaching Tantra*,

> First, in order to halt attachment
> Related to body, speech, and mind,
> Begin the preliminary practice.

Accordingly, it is necessary to do the separation practice related to body, speech, and mind. So, first there is the separation practice related to the body.

a) Separation Practice Related to the Body

The meaning of "one's body moves and twists in different ways" is given in the *Word-Transcending Root Tantra*:

> For the body, all kinds of activities have been taught:
> Moving around, staying still,
> Twisting and moving in different ways,
> Extending and retracting one's limbs.
> Vividly bringing them to mind,
> Mentally act out and use the body to perform
> The physical activities of the six classes of beings.

In order to turn away naturally from all activities with the three doors produced by karma and habitual tendencies and be prevented thereafter from doing them, you should go to an isolated place where no one can see or hear you—this is to avoid the fault of violating the samaya concerning secret conduct or the seventh root downfall. So as not to irritate the good or bad spirits in that place, offer the *serkyem* and torma and entrust them with the activities. After that, you should arouse the bodhicitta, thinking, "For the sake of sentient beings, who fill the whole of space, I will train in the rushen practice of separating samsara and nirvana and subsequently bring all of them to buddhahood." Strip naked and mentally act out the heat and cold of the hells, the hunger and thirst of the hungry spirits, the dullness and stupidity of the animals, the human sufferings of birth, aging, sickness, and death, the demigods' sufferings from fighting and quarreling, the gods' sufferings of transmigration and downfall, and so on, imagining all these as if you were experiencing them yourself. Then, mentally act out and physically train again and again in the whole range of activities— that is, all the physical activities of the six classes of beings, their physical postures and expressions, along with running, staying still, jumping, twisting, extending and retracting their limbs, and so on.

b) Separation Practice Related to Speech

Next, for the rushen separation practice related to speech, the *Word-Transcending Root Tantra* explains the meaning of "one's speech utters the sounds of the different kinds of beings" as follows:

> In order to reverse and annul the things one has said,
> Utter the different sounds, beautiful or unpleasant,
> Of the gods, the nāgas, yakṣas,
> Gandharvas, kumbhāṇḍas,[22] and Viṣṇu.
> In short, imagine and give voice to
> The sounds of the six classes of beings.

Accordingly, without any acceptance or rejection, utter the different sounds and noises by which each of the six classes of beings express themselves—wailing, making war cries, and so forth. This is the separation practice related to speech.

c) Separation Practice Related to Mind

The meaning of "one's mind imagines all kinds of thoughts, both good and bad, uninhibitedly" is to be found in *Only Child of the Buddhas*:

> Delight, disgust, happiness and pain,
> Permanence, impermanence, and the rest,
> Thoughts of the view, meditation, and conduct,
> Thoughts of Dharma and thoughts profane,
> Attachment, aversion, and bewilderment,
> Virtue, evil, and so on—
> Carry out every kind of mental activity.

Accordingly, let all kinds of thoughts occur, bringing to mind the most fantastic ideas, and deliberately let all the memories and thoughts related to past, present, and future, good or bad, come and go.

At the end, when your body, speech, and mind are exhausted— your body is worn out, your voice is speechless, and the thread of the thoughts in your mind is severed—the clingings related to your three doors stop by themselves, and as your mind becomes free of any reference point, take rest in the moment that follows, preserving your own nature, the inconceivable and inexpressible fundamental nature of things.

Similarly, it is said in the *Testament* that one should "practice the conduct of the Three Jewels," meaning that one should train one's body and speech in different ways. With your body, adopt the seven-point posture of Vairocana, emanate and reabsorb rays of light from the coil of hair between the eyebrows, recite the profound sūtras, and in like manner adopt the stance of a wrathful deity, display the nine modes of dance, and so forth. And with your voice, utter the sound of the *rulu* mantra, and *hūṁ phaṭ*, and so on.

4) The Inner Purification by Burning Up the Seeds of the Six
Realms

> Inwardly, in the crown, throat, heart,
> Navel, secret center, and soles of the feet of one's
>   body,
> Within spheres of light of the six colors,
> Are the seeds of the six realms: *a, su, nṛ*,[23] *tri, pre,*
>   and *du*.
> In the centers related to the three doors
> Are the syllables of the three kāyas of all the
>   buddhas,
> A white *oṃ*, red *āḥ*, and blue *hūṃ*,
> Each shining with brilliant rays of light.
> The fire from them consumes without trace
> The seeds and tendencies of the six realms.
> For each of these, one hundred thousand recitations
>   are made,
> Along with the supplement.

In *Luminous Expanse* we read,

> In the crown, throat, heart,
> Navel, secret center, and soles of the feet
> Are located the syllables *a, su, nṛ, tri, pre,* and *du*.

On the inner level, from the moment this body of ours is produced,
the seeds that propel us into the six realms are continuously present
as the afterglow of our previous lives and the perpetuating causes
of our future lives. And when we die, as the wind-mind gathers
in one or other of the channels related to these seed syllables, we
are propelled into the associated realm. Now that we are on the
path, therefore, we use the following method to purify them. It is
particular to the unsurpassable vehicle, with its numerous skillful
methods and lack of difficulty.

The seeds to be purified are as follows. In the crown center is the seed syllable of the gods, a white *a*. In the throat center is the seed syllable of the demigods, a yellowish-green *su*. In the heart center is the seed syllable of the human realm, a light-blue *nṛ*. In the navel center is the seed syllable of the animal realm, a dark-red *tri*. In the secret center is the seed syllable of the hungry spirits, an ash-colored *pre*. And in the soles of the feet are the seed syllables of the hell realms, smoke-colored *du*. Located in spheres of light of their respective colors, these seeds of the six realms, the syllables *a*, *su*, *nṛ*, *tri*, *pre*, and *du*, are what have to be purified.

As for what purifies them, the *Testament* says,

> Because this body is engendered, caused by ignorance,
> The six migrations lie indeed in their seed syllables.
> Because awareness is indeed the triple kāya,
> [The three kāyas also manifest in their three syllables.]
> In these syllables train yourself
> And apply the separating rushen practice.

The purifiers, then, are the self-cognizing primordial wisdom of all the buddhas in the ten directions and three times—the three kāyas, by nature the three vajras, manifesting in the form of syllables, which are visualized in the centers related to one's own three doors. In the crown center is a white *oṃ*, in the throat center a red *āḥ*, and in the heart center a blue *hūṃ*. Visualize these three syllables inconceivably bright, shining with rays of light. From them rays of light—white, red, and blue—emanate upward and touch the sugatas. Consider that, as a result, all the wisdom and qualities of the inexhaustible wheel of ornaments related to their bodies— and likewise all the wisdom and qualities of their speech, minds, qualities, activities, and so on—are gathered in the form of white, red, and blue rays of light and dissolve again and again into the three seed syllables in your own three centers. Then, from the three syllables in your three centers light emanates in the form of fire, flaring up like the flames at the end of the kalpa, with extremely hot tips. It touches your six centers, burning up, without trace, the seeds of the six realms along with the karmic deeds, defilements, and habitual tendencies that produce them, like chaff touched by fire. Visualizing this, recite the three syllables. You should recite the three syllables one hundred thousand times for each of the seeds to be purified, making six hundred thousand recitations, to which it is important to add a supplement of one hundred thousand to make up for errors, which means reciting them seven hundred thousand times in all.

At the end, the fiery mass of wisdom light spreads further and further, burning up the world and beings along with your own body, aggregates, and senses-and-fields. Consider that your body becomes empty yet appearing, like a rainbow, shining like the reflection of the moon on water; and the whole of the three worlds becomes a mass of light, open and free in the all-pervasive, even expanse of the three kāyas, in which there is no possibility of delusion. This is how Dudjom Lingpa taught it.

5) The Guiding Instructions in Terms of the Ordinary Mind, Showing the Methods for Purifying the Three Doors

> To purify the body, one meditates on a vajra in a blazing mass of fire.
> To purify the speech, one intones *hūṁ* quietly and forcefully.
> To purify the mind, one examines where the mind originates, stays, and goes.

a) Purification of the Body

"To purify the body, one meditates on a vajra in a blazing mass of fire" refers to the vajra stance. Stand up with your toes firmly on the ground and the soles of your feet joined together, your knees spread out to the side. With your lower back kept straight, hold your two hands, palms joined, above your head, but not touching it, and spread your elbows. Tuck your chin in.[24] In this pose visualize your body as a three-pronged blue vajra, blazing with fire. Expressing this vocally as well, stand in that position for as long as you can. When you can no longer hold it, consider that your awareness in the form of a white *A* shoots up far into the sky above your head. As you cry *ha*, let your body collapse onto your back like a felled tree.

With regard to the symbolism of purity that needs to be kept in mind, according to the tradition of Omniscient Drime Özer,[25] the three upper prongs of the vajra symbolize the nature, character, and cognizant potency; the three lower prongs symbolize the three kāyas; and the waist joins them together, symbolizing that the combination of primordial purity and spontaneous presence is used as the path. When you are tired of this, adopt the unchanging vajra posture.

The intended purpose of each aspect of this profound practice for purifying the body is explained in the orally transmitted teachings of the Heruka Dudjom Dorje, as follows. As a result of keeping the main body straight, the thought-moving wind is blocked. As a result of keeping the soles of the feet together, the male, female, and neutral winds are emptied, and one realizes luminosity. As a result of directing the two heels at the secret center, the ground of attachment is emptied, and the habitual tendencies of defilements are purified. By joining the palms of one's hands together above one's head, one masters the key point of the body and thus restores the channels and winds to their own natural condition. This is the purpose of this practice.

It creates the right physical connections for realization to dawn in the mind—meaning that by exhausting the body and so on, the threads of thoughts and feelings will be cut and the primordial wisdom dwelling in oneself will manifest nakedly. Moreover, as a result of seeing one's body as a blazing vajra, obstacles from negative forces and obstacle makers are removed, and clinging related to the impure body, speech, and mind naturally ceases; the subtle habitual tendencies of the three doors are purified; the meaning of the three aspects of purification, perfection, and maturation [of the generation stage]²⁶ is assimilated; and ultimately one is freed on the level of the three kāyas.

When you are engaged in practices such as these separation practices related to the three doors, there is something you should never forget—that is, to arouse the bodhicitta so that all sentient beings may attain the level of total freedom, lasting happiness, buddhahood. And at the same time, you should imagine that from the ultimate expanse the very nature of the blessings and wisdom of the body, speech, mind, qualities, and activities of all the tathāgatas appears in the form of five-colored rays of light and dissolves into your three doors, as a result of which the karma and defilements arising from your past deeds and present circumstances and all the evil, obscurations, sufferings, habitual tendencies, and your body of flesh created by them gradually dissolve into the expanse of the great emptiness that is ultimate reality. Then rest in meditative equipoise for a while in the ineffable state of equality, awareness-emptiness. It is very important to apply this to all your practice.

b) Purification of Speech

Next, there is the purification of speech: "To purify the speech, one intones *hūṁ* quietly and forcefully." For this, the *Word-Transcending Root Tantra* states,

> For the speech, there is the practice of *hūṁ*.
> By placing the seal, developing the technique,
> Achieving mental suppleness, and journeying on the road,
> One's speech is purified, bringing benefit to the mind.

i) Placing the Seal

Placing the seal has two parts.

(A) Placing the Seal on Outer Appearances

Go to an isolated place, and maintaining the attitude of the mind set on supreme enlightenment, from a *hūṃ* in your heart center emanate numerous letters *hūṃ* like sparks thrown out from a fire. As the whole realm of the outwardly appearing world and its inner animate contents transforms into *hūṃ*s, softly chant *hūṃ*, your teeth and lips not quite touching, and, mingling the breath, consciousness, and the appearance of *hūṃ*, recite undistractedly. When, as a result of reciting like this, all appearances manifest vividly as *hūṃ*, this is the sign of success in placing the seal. It is said that the purpose of this is to render all appearances open and free in lacking true existence.

(B) Placing the Seal on One's Own Body

All the *hūṃ*s that have emanated outside are gradually, one by one, gathered back. They enter you through your mouth, filling the inside of your body with a jumble of *hūṃ*s. Your body takes on the form of the letter *hūṃ*. At the end, the *hūṃ* letters fade away like a rainbow. Rest at ease, then, in the state of the dharmadhātu, free from elaboration.

The purpose of these practices is as follows. By placing the seal on outer appearances, clinging to sense objects is halted, and one directly experiences the fundamental nature, the lack of intrinsic existence in appearing objects. And by placing the seal on one's own body, the elements of one's body are purified, and its solidity dissolves into its pristine condition.

ii) Developing the Technique

Developing the technique has two parts.

(A) Developing the Technique with Regard to Outer Appearances

For this, you should repeat *hūṁ hūṁ* very forcefully and consider that, as a result, powerful, sharp, swift, dark-blue *hūṁ*s appear like thunderbolts. They pierce all the mountain ranges, rocks, and buildings, passing in and out, completely unimpeded, leaving nothing substantial. In brief, all the appearances of the billionfold universe are purified—destroyed and rendered empty. Remain in meditative equipoise in the state of awareness-emptiness free of elaboration. The purpose of this is to recognize appearances as lacking true existence.

(B) Developing the Technique with Regard to One's Body

Again, a dark-blue letter *hūṁ* a span[27] in size appears and passes back and forth through your body. Consider that it passes in and out from the tips of the hair on your head to the soles of your feet, destroying everything, and forcefully recite *hūṁ*. A sign of successful training in this is that one's body comes out in goose bumps and feels insubstantial, like a reflection in a mirror. As a result of this practice, on a temporary level, sicknesses, negative spirits, and obstacles are removed, and on the ultimate level, one's body matures into a body of light and is freed, inseparable from the vajra body of all the conquerors.

iii) Achieving Mental Suppleness

Sit cross-legged on a comfortable seat and place in front of you a straight stick. Visualize in your heart center a dark-blue *hūṁ*, the nature of wind and mind combined, shining brightly. From it, countless azure-blue letters *hūṁ* like sparks emitted from a fire, emerge in a continuous chain, one after another. It reaches the foot of the stick in front that you are using as the support for your concentration, and at the same time the first letter *hūṁ* starts to spiral clockwise up to the top of the stick, the others following suit, like a snake entwining itself round the stick. When the first letter *hūṁ* reaches the top of the stick, keep it firmly there. Concentrating on this, chant *hūṁ* softly.

After that, the *hūṁs* come back the same way from the top of the stick. Dissolving one into the other, along with the *hūṁ* that was at the top of the stick, they are gathered into the *hūṁ* in your heart center. Rest at ease in the nonconceptual state. Train in this way, alternating the forward emanation outward and the return dissolution inward. The purpose of this is to achieve a fully supple mind, to give rise to extraordinary qualities in one's mindstream, and to be able to transform any kind of object.

iv) Journeying on the Road

Manifesting your body as a *hūṁ*, visualize a span-sized, dark-blue letter *hūṁ* radiating light and rays of light. Imagine that it sets off, twisting here and there in worm fashion up to a cubit above the ground without touching it. It travels all over the earth to the mountains and lands that you can see and those that you know about but cannot see, like an eager tourist taking to the road. As you concentrate on this, softly chant *hūṁ*, matching the recitation to the pace of your travels.

Again, gradually wander throughout the lands and abodes of the six classes of beings. And with the rays of light from the *hūṁ*, purify all the beings in the six realms, cleansing them of their respective karmic perceptions, sufferings, and habitual tendencies, like sunlight falling on darkness, and bringing them to the level of total freedom. Dissolving dualistic appearances—samsaric apprehension—into the ultimate expanse, rest at ease in the expanse of the great equality, free of duality.

After that, as you recite *hūṁ hūṁ*, imagine that the *hūṁ* travels like a skilled archer's arrow to the pure buddha fields such as the buddha field of Manifest Joy in the east. This will create the connections for attaining such buddha fields.

Keeping breath, consciousness, and *hūṁ* combined together in all this is a very powerful method for stopping discursive thoughts. The purpose of this practice is to purify obscurations related to speech and attain freedom in the saṃbhogakāya.

c) Purification of the Mind

"To purify the mind, one examines where the mind originates, stays, and goes." This is explained in the *Word-Transcending Root Tantra*:

> If one investigates where, in the first place, the mind originates,
> Where, in the meantime, it stays, and where, in the end, it goes,
> One will purify the mind and know its fundamental nature.

In the first place, there is no origin from which this mind appears: mind is emptiness. In the meanwhile, there is nowhere that it stays: it is emptiness. In the end, there is nowhere that it goes: it is emptiness. This is the conclusion one needs to make. As this point is explained in detail below, I will not enlarge on it here. In short, the purpose of purifying the mind is to cleanse mental obscurations, remove obstacles, reverse clinging, and make the mind subside in primordial wisdom, aware and empty.

6) Relaxing the Three Doors in Their Natural State

> One should relax one's three doors in their natural
> state to render them fit.
> The key point of the body is to adopt the seven-point
> posture of the path of liberation.
> The key point of the speech is to expel the air nine
> times and train in the wind.

> The key point of the mind is to develop the
> motivation of compassion for all beings.
> One should pray to the teacher, mingle one's
> mind with the teacher's, and receive the four
> empowerments.

This verse, it would seem, is indicating the meaning of both relaxing in the natural state and refreshing oneself together.[28]

For a general presentation of relaxing in the natural state, the *Word-Transcending Root Tantra* says,

> At this time, the key points related to body, speech, and mind
> Are for the practitioner to leave them in their natural state.

If the preliminary practices result in your constitution and elements being disturbed, it is important to relax in the natural state. Therefore, go to a pleasant place where your meditation will not be disturbed and remain like a human corpse in a charnel ground, neither adopting nor avoiding physical activity, good or bad. With regard to your speech, you should remain like a lute with broken strings or a person who cannot speak. And your mind should be left in a state free of elaboration, like a cloudless sky. This is what we call, "relaxing in the natural state."

Next is refreshing yourself. Having relaxed your three doors in their natural state, you should settle in uncontrived naturalness. This is the unmistaken means for rendering one's body, speech, and mind fit. Consequently, the key point for the body is to sit in the seven-point posture of the path of liberation: both legs crossed, the two hands in the meditation gesture, spine straight, eyes focused along the tip of the nose, neck slightly bent, tongue touching the palate, and breath left to settle naturally.

The key point of the speech is to expel the impure wind. How to train in the pure wisdom wind and so on can be found in other texts. In brief, expel the stale air nine times.

Then, for the key point of the mind, you should develop the correct motivation: reflect on how the sentient beings of the six realms, who have been your parents, are tormented by innumerable different kinds of suffering, the result of the three or five poisons, and so on. And develop compassion for them until it feels unbearable.

After that, it is here that the view of the Great Perfection is introduced. There are three ways in which this can be done: the way of the view gained by receiving teachings and reflecting; the way of meditation on the pith instructions; and the way of the transfer of blessings. It is the last of these three that is presented here, and it depends exclusively on the practice of guru yoga. Cultivate pure perception, seeing the teacher as the Buddha in person, and pray to the teacher and mingle your mind and their mind inseparably. From the teacher, take the four empowerments. The purpose of this is to purify the four obscurations and realize the four kāyas. In particular, if the genuine view of the Great Perfection is to take birth in your mindstream, it is necessary for the transfer of blessings to take place. Without pure perception and devotion with regard to the teacher, it is impossible for this to happen, for as the sublime beings of the past have said, "If you have wrong ideas, thinking of the teacher as an ordinary person, you will get no more accomplishment than from a dead dog."

7) Examining Which, of the Body, Speech, and Mind, Is the Most Important

> One should examine whether one's body, speech,
>   and mind
> Are the same or distinct.
> The doer of all things
> Is nothing other than the mind.

Examining your body made of the four elements, your speech that utters all kinds of pleasant and unpleasant sounds, and your mind that gives rise to all your happiness and suffering, investigate whether these three are a same, single entity or three separate things. If they were the same, then when your voice is silent, the body and mind too should be absent. And when you abandon this body, your mind too would be no more. On the other hand, if they are distinct entities, then investigate, which of the three has the greatest influence or is the most important. From time without beginning, each time you take a new birth, your body of the previous existence dissolves into the four elements, and your voice, which has always been associated with your breath, fades away. Yet the mind continues to wander, from the Peak of Existence to the depths of the hell of Torment Unsurpassed, and it will have to continue wandering until the end of endless samsara. Examine how the body and voice, being replaced, are impermanent, while the continuity of the mind is uninterrupted. Even now, when you accumulate the seven unvirtuous deeds with your body and speech, it is the mind that first thinks, "I am going to do that," and puts your body and speech to work. And when you perform the seven virtuous deeds of body and speech, it is the mind that first thinks of them and employs the body and speech as servants. When, as a result of this investigation, you realize that the doer of all deeds is nothing other than the mind, you will necessarily come to the conclusion that the mind is like a king and the body and speech are like its vassals.

8) Looking for Where the Mind Comes From, Dwells, and Goes

> One should investigate the place from where the
>   mind first comes
> And what it is that comes into being;
> Examine the place where the mind, in the
>   meantime, dwells
> And what it is that dwells;
> And look for the place to which, in the end, the
>   mind goes

And what it is that goes.
One should examine in detail whether it has shape
    or color.
In the same way, one should examine the existence
    of appearances.
When one sees that while appearing,
They are devoid of intrinsic existence,
One should examine whether all that is empty is
    luminous.
The character of open emptiness is intrinsically
    luminous.
Since there is no reference point,
One will see unobstructed primordial wisdom.
The mind creates karmic deeds,
And it is the mind that experiences pleasure and
    pain.
The whole variety of phenomena appear to the
    mind:
There is nothing that is not created by the mind.
One should closely investigate the nature of the
    mind
And consider whether seeker and sought are one or
    two.
One should look for an "I" and the clinging to a self.
When one realizes there is none, one will see that
    the clinging to an "I" is rootless.
One should minutely examine that which sees it:
When one realizes that the seer is certainly
    groundless, rootless,
One will see the actual condition of things, beyond
    assertions,
The unborn nature of the path.

First, investigate where the mind comes from. When you do so, you
will find that it does not come from anywhere—not from the four

elements, the universe and its inhabitants (on the outer level); not from one's body, whether from the top, the bottom, or in between (on the inner level); and not from the display of objects and appearances that make up the pleasures of the senses (on the intermediary level). It is devoid of origin. And when you examine the mind that comes into being, you will find that even if, when not examined or analyzed, it appears to exist, if it is examined and analyzed, there is nothing there: it is nothing but the great emptiness, as is stated in a tantra:

> What we call "mind" is the door of multifarious appearances,
> With all kinds of thoughts,
> The ground of all samsara and nirvana.
> It arises, yet from where does it first arise?
> However much, however minutely, one examines
> All the objects that constitute what we know—
> The appearances and imputations related to
> Earth, stone, mountains, rocks,
> And emptiness, nothingness, the expanse of space, and so
> forth—
> They are empty by nature.
> No place of origin of the mind is found in them, and
> nothing to originate.

Similarly, if you further investigate where, in the meantime, this aware and thinking, active thing that we call "mind" dwells, even if you look everywhere—at the objects that appear outside as the world and its inhabitants, or at the inner body (from head to toe and in between)—you will never find a place about which you can say, "This is where the mind dwells." And again, if you examine the nature of the "dweller," the mind itself, you will see that in whatever way it manifests, the moment it manifests, it disappears without trace, like snow falling on hot rock. There is nowhere it dwells and nothing that dwells, as we read in the *Later Tantra of the Expanse of Samantabhadra's Wisdom*:

When one looks for a place where it might dwell—
From the crown of the head to the soles of the feet
Of sentient beings created from habitual tendencies—
The mind that feels manifests as emptiness.

In the same way, if you examine whether there is a place to which, in the end, this thinking, active thing that we call "mind" goes, even if you keep on investigating until this universe is emptied, you will never find anywhere to which the mind goes—not in the earth, stones, mountains, or rocks of the world outside, nor anywhere in your own body inside (from the tips of the hairs on your head to the tips of your toenails), nor in the four cardinal directions, the eight intermediate directions, or the zenith or nadir. And if you look for and examine the goer—the mind itself—past thoughts have ceased and so do not exist, future thoughts have not yet arisen and so do not exist, and the consciousness of the present moment is groundless, rootless, referenceless, and open and unimpeded: it vanishes on its own and therefore has no ground.

Thus, the nature of the mind is, from the very beginning, devoid of arising, ceasing, and staying. Even the cognitions of the apprehended object and apprehending subject that appear as mind and mental factors are cleared away in a nonreferential state. The nature of the mind is devoid of all assertions, ineffable, inexpressible, and inconceivable. It is the groundless, rootless nature pervading the whole of samsara and nirvana, the ultimate, fundamental condition that is the unborn dharmakāya. To understand this directly is the result of examining where the mind comes from, where it dwells, and where it goes.

When one investigates in this way, one realizes that the mind has no origin and no location, so the mind's deceptive structures collapse. One reaches the definite conclusion that since it has nowhere to go, the objects that appear are mental fabrications. One gains the confidence that because there is nothing that goes, the subject is devoid of intrinsic existence.

These lines in the root text constitute a pith instruction that subsumes the teachings on the mind's lack of origin, location, and destination and causes the inner sanctum of the mind to collapse. It is thus an extraordinarily profound pith instruction.

Now, if you investigate further, with regard to the mind's shape, you will find that the mind is not a form, so it cannot exist as any of the eight different kinds of shapes.[29] And if you scrutinize it to see whether or not it has a color, you will see that it does not exist as any of the primary colors or the eight secondary tones.[30] The mind is devoid of shape and color. It is emptiness, free of all conceptual extremes—existence, nonexistence, both, neither, and so on. This line resolves the question of the apprehending mind, the subject.

Similarly, investigate the existence, or otherwise, of everything that manifests in the form of objects of apprehension—the vast container (the universe) that appears outside, its innumerable contents (sentient beings) that exist inside, and the beautiful array of appearances related to the five pleasure of the senses that move in between.

Even though, unexamined, the appearances of the world, beings, and sense pleasures appear, they do not exist as such. They are devoid of intrinsic being. They are groundless and rootless—just as the things you actually saw with your eyes in last night's dream, the objects you held in your hands, the things that manifested to your senses, and so forth appeared to exist, yet today, as the experiences in your dream have vanished, you realize that those appearances of last night's dream never existed.

When you see that since they are by nature referenceless, and open and unimpeded, they are empty, you will conclude that all the things of phenomenal existence, samsara and nirvana, are empty. This emptiness is not a nonaffirming negation or a sole emptiness. Nor is it a void nihilistic blank or a vacant mind, as in the view of Hashang; nor like a sustained calm devoid of thoughts. Rather, all that is empty, while empty by nature, is at the same time intrinsically luminous. What one first has to examine and decide is whether or not the nature of phenomena is luminosity and emptiness inseparable. The emptiness that is established as the nature of all the phenomena of samsara and nirvana, in that they have no existence whatsoever, is not a pitch-black or dark state as when one is in deep sleep or unconscious. Luminosity and emptiness are inseparable, so appearances can manifest in every possible way, as is stated in the *Tantra of the Self-Arising Fundamental Nature*:

> Anything can manifest in every kind of way.
> There is no obstruction to what appears,
> As in a perfectly clean mirror.

Thus, where the root text states, "The character of open emptiness is intrinsically luminous," the Great Oḍḍiyāna[31] says,

> The character of emptiness is intrinsic luminosity,
> Its radiance is unceasing cognizant potency . . .

Accordingly, he speaks of the "naturally luminous intrinsic nature," "naturally luminous self-cognizing awareness," and "naturally luminous character." Similarly, Mipham Rinpoche says,

> Even though there is nothing to see and we cannot see anything, we speak of "luminosity" shining from the depths. Rest in that state that is luminous yet transparently empty, empty yet luminous—emptiness-luminosity, free from grasping.

Since there is absolutely no object or reference point, if you settle in meditative equipoise in that state, you will see directly the very face of uncontrived, self-arisen primordial wisdom, unobstructed luminosity-emptiness.

All the appearances of samsara and nirvana, then, are empty, but with regard to emptiness, it is not as if there is no tea and no water. In truth, they are, by nature, nothing but the one sole sphere, ceaseless awareness, empty and luminous. However, when the causes and conditions come together—namely, the clinging to a self that all the sentient beings in the three worlds of samsara have, and their conceptual thoughts—all the hallucinatory appearances of the three worlds manifest, even though they do not exist. Consequently, mental activity leads to the creation of all kinds of positive and negative deeds, and these result in the whole variety of pleasurable, painful, and neutral perceptions that are experienced in the mind like never ending ripples on water. Thus, what creates the positive and negative karmic deeds is the mind, and what experiences their result is the mind.

In this way, although the appearances of the oceanlike sphere of phenomena—the diverse appearances that are the objects of the six senses, and so on—have, from the very beginning, never existed, despite being nonexistent, to the mind they do appear to exist. And when the mind grasps at those appearances as truly existing, there is delusion. And delusion is as limitless as appearances, for as Shabkar says,

> The inanimate appearances of the universe are the mind,
> The six classes of beings that inhabit it are the mind,
> The happiness of celestial and human beings in the higher
>   realms are the mind,
> And the sufferings in the three lower realms too are the
>   mind.

Indeed, there is nothing in existence that is not fashioned by the mind, as is affirmed in the *All-Illuminating Sphere Tantra*:

> All the buddhas of the three times were created by the
>   mind,
> All the beings in the three worlds were created by the mind.

You might wonder, then: What is the nature of the mind itself—this mind that creates everything? Investigate the mind's nature from all angles: Is it existent, nonexistent, both or neither; is it exclusive or inclusive; is it one or various? And so on. When you do so, you will understand that it is the great equality beyond mental elaboration, which does not exist in any way. When you look for the mind's shape, color, features, size, aspects, and so on, you will find there is nothing existent that apprehends or is apprehended, a seeker or anything to be sought. It cannot be described in words or in imagination. It is beyond all assertions, for it is groundless and rootless.

This sort of realization constitutes the profound view of the Middle Way, as expressed in this and other passages from *Refutation of Criticisms*:

> I have no assertions.
> Therefore, I am not at fault.

And,

> Moreover, when there are no assertions and no
>   philosophical tenets,
> That is the Great Middle Way.

Accordingly, the ultimate views of the Great Seal, Great Perfection, and Great Middle Way are established of necessity as being one and the same.

By investigating and looking for the mind in this way, both the seeker and what is being sought will disintegrate without trace, like a design drawn on water. When, for example, a ship sinks, if you try and hold onto the water, there is nothing to hold onto. Similarly, when the seeker investigates itself, there is nothing to support it and therefore nothing to identify. The mind does not tend toward any aspect—outer or inner, container or content, appearance or emptiness, existence or nonexistence. So you have to accept that it does not exist in any way, as one or two, and so on. For as it is said,

> It is not single: it knows and manifests in multiple ways.
> It is not multiple: it is one inseparable taste.

Similarly, as the root text says, "One should look for an 'I' and the clinging to a self." There are two kinds of clinging to a self: the clinging to an individual self and the clinging to a self in phenomena. The first of these is the belief that there is a truly existent so-called "self" that one identifies with one's body, speech, and mind.[32] The clinging to a self in phenomena is the notion that all the multifarious phenomena comprising the outer world and its inhabitants exist truly inasmuch as they exist as the objects that one sees, hears, and thinks. The remedies for these two beliefs are the view that realizes the absence of self in the individual and the view that realizes the absence of self in phenomena.

With regard to the first of these, if you look for the self using your intellect to dissect all the constituents of your body—the flesh, blood, bones, internal organs, skin, and body hair—you cannot but conclude that there is no self in the body. Similarly, if you look for a self in all the pleasant and unpleasant things you say, you will conclude that there is no self in your speech. If you look for a self or the absence of a self in the positive, negative, and neutral thoughts in your mind, you will conclude that there is no self in your mind. And you have also to conclude that neither is there a self distinct from and adjacent to the body, speech, and mind, like a foal standing next to an adult horse. Thus, what we call the "self" does not exist as either something that is the same as the three doors or one that is distinct from them. To realize that it is empty, an open and unimpeded state of equality free of conceptual elaboration, is the view of the realization of no-self in the individual.

Secondly, when you reduce the gross phenomena that make up the world and its inhabitants to their subtle constituents, and likewise reduce the subtle constituents to their different parts, the parts to indivisible atoms, the indivisible atoms to a nonreferential state, and the nonreferential state to emptiness, you will realize that the phenomenal self is open, unimpeded emptiness devoid of anything whatsoever, the great equality beyond mental elaboration. This is what we call the view of the realization of no-self in phenomena.

When you gain a correct understanding that both kinds of clinging to a self do not exist in any way and are but the display of great emptiness, you will see that the so-called clinging to "I," or self-clinging, is groundless and rootless—you will see the fundamental nature of things.

If you now minutely examine the consciousness that sees this, you will realize that the partless instants of consciousness too are nothing other than the great emptiness. Thus the consciousness that sees this is certainly groundless and rootless, a nonreferential open and unimpeded play. When you realize this, you will see the nature as it is, the fundamental nature of the path Great Perfection, unborn, empty awareness.

9) Distinguishing Mind and Awareness

> The universal ground is the ground
> Of the whole of samsara and nirvana;
> It is a latent state that remains indeterminate.
> It is the ground from which the eight consciousnesses,
> The twenty lesser defilements, and other mental factors,
> And every single thought proliferate.
> The dharmakāya is like clear, unclouded water,
> Free of delusion, beyond the realm of the elaborations
> Of apprehending subject and apprehended object.
> The mind and awareness are like ice and water:
> Their nature is the same, but conditions make them
>   different.
> The mind is virtuous thoughts—faith and renunciation—
> And attachment and aversion to friends and foes,
>   and indifference.

The difference between the universal ground and the dharmakāya is as follows. The universal ground is the source or ground of existence—that is, of all the deluded perceptions of the six classes of beings that appear as samsara. And it is the source or ground of peace—that is, of all the appearances of the four kāyas and five wisdoms in nirvana. It is a latent state of consciousness that remains in an indeterminate state that is neither virtuous nor unvirtuous. Jigme Lingpa describes it in *Distinguishing Three Key Points* as follows:

> The universal ground is the ground of all samsara and
>   nirvana.
> It is like murky water:
> The latent tendencies of bewilderment and confusion
> Hide the clarity of primordial wisdom, awareness.

Where the text says, "The mind and awareness are like ice and water," awareness is unceasing emptiness-clarity, the clarity aspect, like, for example, perfectly clear water. As Omniscient Jigme Lingpa says,

> Awareness is like pure water cleared of cloudiness:
> It has the nature of being rid of adventitious contaminants.
> It is the essence of all the qualities of perfect freedom—
> It is primordial wisdom that henceforth cannot know
>   delusion.

As for the mind, it pursues the object and is contaminated by the object, like a drop of water that has fallen on some earth. It has references and goals. It manifests unpredictably as all sorts of thoughts flashing back and forth, knowing this and that, thinking this and that. On and on it goes, never finished, never staying still, ever thinking, ever imagining. As Shabkar says,

> What we call the mind is ever knowing, ever thinking.
> Try to chase it, you will never catch it; it is fugitive and
>   evanescent.
> Try to keep it still, it will not stay; it flits here and there, ever
>   restless.

And in *Distinguishing Three Key Points* we read,

> The mind zigzags from one object to another
> Or is obsessed with one thing,
> Or uncontrollably blown about,
> Based on a variety of conditions.

The nature of both mind and awareness is but unceasing knowing, uncompounded, empty and luminous. However, as a result of the clinging to self (the cause) and of thoughts (the conditions), awareness transforms into a dualistic mind that apprehends subject and object. The mind is virtuous thoughts (faith, devotion and respect, determination to be free, and the mind set on enlightenment), unvirtuous thoughts (thoughts of attachment, aversion, and ignorance with regard to friend and foe), and neutral thoughts of indifference. Consequently the mind has become the ground from which the eight gatherings of consciousness, the fifty mental factors such as the twenty lesser defilements, and every one of the eighty-four thousand kinds of thoughts proliferate.

Awareness, or the dharmakāya, is like pure water cleared of cloudiness, as is stated in *Distinguishing Three Key Points*:

> The dharmakāya is like water cleared of cloudiness.

Awareness, or the dharmakāya, is characterized by unclouded clarity, completely untainted by drowsiness, dullness, and gloom or by wild thoughts. It is devoid of the contaminants of delusion, beyond the realm of the elaborations of apprehending subject and apprehended object. And three definite assertions can be made about it: it has never been deluded in the past, it is not deluded at present, and there is no possibility of it ever being deluded in the future.

B) A Specific Explanation of the Main Practice, the Introduction to the Nature of Awareness

The introduction to the nature of awareness has two sections: (1) showing the fundamental nature of awareness and (2) showing the means for making awareness manifest. The first of these is divided into six parts.[33]

1) Showing the Fundamental Nature of Awareness
a) Differences between the Relative and Ultimate and Distinctions between Knowledge and Ignorance

> Genuine awareness, the essence that is luminosity,
> Sees samsara and nirvana like space, open and
>   unimpeded.
> Although, if one elaborates, there are infinite
>   distinctions
> Such as the differences between relative and
>   ultimate,
> One should examine the difference between
>   realization and lack of realization,
> Knowledge and ignorance,[34]
> To determine what is the fundamental nature.

The nature of the mind is the primordial wisdom of luminosity—this is the essence of the eighty-four thousand aspects of the Dharma. It is, as it were, the butter churned from the milk of the sacred Dharma. This authentic awareness is like space, as is stated in the *Tantra of the All-Creating King*:

> My nature is like space, a metaphor for all,
> Nobody can alter pure space,
> Pure space cannot be altered by anybody.
> Space is beyond all action, effort, and practice.

Self-cognizing awareness is beyond effortful practice, alteration, or contamination. When one settles in meditative equipoise in that state of awareness, which is free from all elaborations such as outer and inner, periphery and center, directions and intermediate directions, one should recognize everything that manifests as its creative power and display as being the single, self-arisen awareness, without using any effortful practice involving rejection or adoption. There is nothing else to do than this. As Guru Padmasambhava's disciple Palgyi Yeshe said,

> The self-arisen primordial wisdom transcends the ordinary mind.
> The nature of the mind is without periphery or center, like space.
> The perceptions of the eight consciousnesses cannot be identified.
> The self-arisen wisdom mind is just this.

And in the *Tantra of the All-Creating King* we read,

> All things are the enlightened mind,
> And as one example serves for all,
> They are by nature like space;
> The meaning of enlightened mind is like that too.

Thus self-arisen awareness, luminosity, is nothing other than space-like in nature, and therefore all the phenomena of samsara and nirvana that manifest through its creative power and display are seen as space-like, open and unimpeded, devoid of all elaboration. In that state, one completely lets go. There is nothing else to do than relax.

Generally speaking, from the relative, deluded point of view, the impure, deluded appearances of the six realms, from the Peak of Existence down to Torment Unsurpassed, seem to be true, to exist, to be present—and there is no end to the ways in which this is expressed. But from the ultimate, undeluded point of view, these appearances of samsara and nirvana have, from the very beginning, never been there. They have never existed. There has never been any delusion. There has never been any movement from the ground.

To discuss these differences in greater detail, there are countless different ways of distinguishing them, but they boil down to the following distinctions. If one has realized the view of the fundamental nature, one is a buddha; if one has not realized it, one is a sentient being. If one knows exactly how the true nature is, one is free; if one does not know it, one is deluded.

One should begin by examining such differences with discriminating logic, by hearing and reflecting on the teachings, to determine what is the fundamental nature. In the end, all the differences between nirvana (purity and freedom) and samsara (impurity and lack of freedom) are simply the difference between knowledge[35] and ignorance, as we find in a tantra:

> If we know thatness, we attain buddhahood.
> If we do not, we wander, deluded, in samsara.

And Longchenpa says,

> Even though from one awareness self-cognizing,
> Nirvana and samsara both arise,
> Their root is one, the ultimate enlightened mind.
> The difference that divides them
> Derives from the recognition or nonrecognition of
> awareness.[36]

And the *Tantra of the Self-Arising Fundamental Nature* has,

> In this way, all appearing phenomena
> In their different transformations
> Are inseparable within dharmatā.
> Rest in meditative evenness in that inseparability.

Thus, the transformations or otherwise of samsara and nirvana, their recognition or otherwise, are—apart from being like the front and back of the hand—no different.

b) Introducing Awareness That Is the Three Kāyas, Free of Thoughts Related to the Three Times

> When one leaves the five sense consciousnesses
> In the natural flow without manipulating them,
> Without projecting or gathering thoughts, rejecting
> or accepting,
> After the first thought has manifested and disappeared
> And in the instant before the next thought arises,
> There is awareness of the present moment, fresh and
> naked.
> Its nature, empty from the beginning, is the
> dharmakāya.
> Its character, unobscured, is the saṃbhogakāya.
> Its cognizant power, manifesting ceaselessly, is the
> nirmāṇakāya.

The first two lines indicate explicitly the way to settle the mind. The ways to settle the body and speech should be understood as being indicated implicitly. So, to begin with, the method for settling the body is to sit with legs crossed, with both hands in the gesture of finding rest in the nature of the mind, the spine kept straight, and the eyes looking straight ahead into space.

Second, the method for settling the speech is as described by Shabkar:

> The key point for the breath is to breathe not through the
> nose but through the mouth.
> With teeth and lips slightly parted,
> Breathe in and out very gently.
> This, the key point for the breath, is most important.

And Dodrub Jigme Tenpa'i Nyima says,

> If the moving karmic wind settles in its natural state,
> the wind related to thoughts and defilements becomes
> naturally clear, and when that happens, the wind of
> primordial wisdom—that is, awareness—gathers in the
> expanse [of the central channel, or *uma*]. This is a special
> feature of this path.

Third, the method for settling the mind is as follows. Without in
any way trying to correct or modify, reject or accept, or prevent or
achieve anything in relation to the five sense consciousnesses, leave
them in the uncontrived natural flow. Do not project thoughts outward; do not draw them in. Without rejecting or accepting or fix-
ating on any appearances that manifest, let go and relax in a serene
state of spaciousness. This is how to settle the mind.

In this way, relax and leave the body perfectly still, like a mountain. Relax and leave all verbal expression in a state of silence, as
when an echo has died out. And for the mind—all thoughts, good
and bad, let them be, and stay relaxed, carefree, in a state beyond
expression or imagination.

Once you are settled like this, do not pursue the past, initial
thoughts, which have already manifested and disappeared. Do not
welcome the next, future thoughts in this instant when they have
not yet arisen. As the consciousness of the present moment dissolves by itself, what is left is the awareness aspect—inexpressible
awareness, clear and empty—fresh and naked like husked grain.
Drawn from the sheath of the tattered clothes of past, present, and
future thoughts, this naked, uncontaminated, open and unimpeded awareness, like a crystal ball, is the wisdom mind of all the
buddhas of the three times, the heart blood of the hundred thousand mother ḍākinīs, the quintessence of the eighty-four thousand
approaches to the Dharma. It is like a core from which all the tantras have arisen, a distillate of all the pith instructions, a digest of
the key points of all the buddhas' teachings. It is the king of views,

which we call the Luminous Great Perfection. Karma Lingpa speaks of it as follows:

> Awareness of the present moment, unobstructed, vivid,
> Is none other than Primordial Lord Samantabhadra.
> The empty expanse that does not exist in any way is
>   Samantabhadrī.
> The moment you realize that, you are a perfect buddha.

And Shabkar declares,

> The moment you settle, there is "ordinary" mind, naked.
> When you look, there is nothing to see—it is pellucid.
> Awareness, pellucid and awake in direct perception,
> Is completely nonexistent, empty and lucid;
> It is the genuine inseparability of luminosity and emptiness.

And Mipham Rinpoche says,

> When you are in the state of awareness, it is as if you
> were watching it. There is nothing to see. But even
> though nothing is seen, deep down, there is luminos-
> ity. Even when there is distraction, its nature does not
> change. Even when there is no distraction, you should
> be free of reference.

Such awareness is by nature empty from the beginning. It is like the sky devoid of the three blemishes.[37] This emptiness is the dhar-makāya. The character of emptiness is its luminosity, free of all obscuring veils. That unobstructed radiance is the saṃbhogakāya. The unceasing multifarious manifestations, as if in a mirror, of its cognizant power constitute the nirmāṇakāya. As Longchenpa says,

> The ground, awareness self-cognizing,
> Is just like a crystal sphere.

Its emptiness is dharmakāya.
Its radiant luminosity is the saṃbhogakāya.
Its unobstructed ground for the unfolding
Is nirmāṇakāya.
The three kāyas in the ground's expanse
Are all spontaneously present.[38]

And,

The changeless and nonreferential dharmakāya
Is infinite and present in all things.
In it is saṃbhogakāya,
Appearances both out and in,
The world and its inhabitants.
The self-arising of phenomena, reflection-like,
Is the nirmāṇakāya.
Therefore, there are no phenomena
That are not perfectly subsumed
As the adornments of the triple kāya.
Everything that manifests is the display
Of the enlightened body, speech, and mind.[39]

The nature of awareness, though not existing in any way, possesses
the potential to manifest in every way. So while awareness never
moves from the expanse of the three kāyas, through its creative
power all the appearances of samsara and nirvana manifest unceasingly. As we find in *The Precious Treasury of the Dharmadhātu,*

Empty by its nature, [luminous in] character,
And unimpeded [in its knowing power],
It does not exist as anything at all—
And anything at all arises from it.
Unbidden, samsara and nirvana both emerge
Within the space of the three kāyas.
And yet from this expanse they do not stray—
The field of blissful ultimate reality.[40]

c) Showing That Awareness, Luminous and Empty, Free of Clinging, Is the One and Only Sphere

> Empty luminosity, luminous emptiness—without
>   any concept of it as such,
> This alert and wakeful [awareness], untainted by
>   thoughts of the past, present, and future,
> Is spoken of as "the one and only sphere of the
>   dharmakāya, transcending mind."

The character of the mind is luminous while its nature is empty. Its spontaneous radiance is indivisibly empty yet luminous. It is not just empty: the character of its emptiness is luminous. Its luminous character has no true existence; the nature of luminosity is emptiness. The nature of awareness, therefore, is luminosity and emptiness inseparable. It is this naked awareness aspect, luminosity and emptiness inseparable, that needs to be realized. But to apprehend luminosity and emptiness as indivisible is not awareness: it is grasping—a conceptual thought—and one must definitely not have that sort of grasping. Awareness, then, is an aware, yet empty and luminous, state free of grasping, uncontaminated by thoughts related to past, present, and future. It is the primordial wisdom that pervades the whole of samsara and nirvana, vast, open, and spacious. In this respect, it is said to be "alert and wakeful." This "alert wakefulness" should not be understood as being a blank, vacant state like the view of Hashang. One should understand it as being a relaxed, spacious state, open and unimpeded, devoid of any reference, as described by Omniscient Longchenpa:

> It is not bound—restricted—by an apprehender.
> It transcends all objects to be apprehended.
> Within it there is nothing that might
> Act as target, nothing to refer to.
> Alert and wakeful, open, undistracted,
> It is the state of wisdom wherein mentation is exhausted—

The sky-like, endless, all-embracing state of evenness
Transcending meditation and the absence of the same:
The great space of Samantabhadra's wisdom.[41]

This sort of awareness is referred to as "the one and only sphere of
the dharmakāya, transcending mind," meaning that the primordial wisdom of the fundamental nature is beyond the sphere of the
intellect. As Śāntideva says,

> The ultimate is not within the reach of intellect,
> For intellect is said to be the relative.[42]

As for the meaning of "the one and only sphere," since this self-
arisen awareness is free of all the edges and corners of thoughts, it
is a "sphere." And since all the appearances of samsara and nirvana
do not go beyond the sphere of awareness, it is "one and only."

d) Introducing Inexpressible Awareness, the Fourth State in Which the Other Three Are Absent

> Genuine awareness, the fourth state in which the
>   other three are absent,
> Is unobstructed, clear, unobscured, limpid,
> A state that is not torpid, that is vivid, unclouded,
>   awake.
> Groundless, rootless, it is devoid of birth and
>   cessation.
> It does not tend to one side or the other
> And is free from the extremes of permanence and
>   discontinuity,
> Unlimited in extent, and beyond coming and going.
> It pervades the whole of samsara and nirvana,
> Yet it is neither one nor various.
> It is free of fixation, without thoughts like "It is this;
>   it is not that."

> Though it cannot be indicated by analogy or word,
> It is as pure as the sky.
> Its own character manifests, openly and unobstructedly.

The "fourth state in which the other three are absent" is the term applied, when one sits relaxed in body, speech, and mind, without contrivance, to a fourth state in which thoughts related to the three times are absent—uncontrived self-arisen awareness, unconcealed and naked, laid bare, bright and limpid. When that state of genuine awareness, the fourth state in which the three are absent, is realized, it is not that all appearances cease and everything goes dark. The objects of the six consciousnesses do not stop appearing. Things appear, various and vivid, just as they do to a child visiting a temple, or when a brocade is spread out, or when one looks at a crowd of people in a courtyard. As it is said,

> To the five senses their five corresponding objects appear
> uninterruptedly.

They manifest clearly without interruption. In *Net of Illusory Manifestations* we read,

> The sublime all-knowing awareness transcends the phe-
> nomenon of consciousness.

And Dudjom Lingpa says,

> Anything can manifest in every kind of way.
> There is no obstruction to what appears,
> As in a perfectly clean mirror.

And,

> Cognizance that knows everything, is aware of every-
> thing, is open and unimpeded . . .

Thus the fundamental state of awareness is unobscured, or has never been clouded, by drowsiness, dullness, and gloom. It is perfectly clear, as is stated in the *Heart Essence of Vairotsana*:

> The hallucinatory appearances of the three worlds of
> samsara
> Have never impaired it: it is open and unimpeded.
> The compassion of the conquerors of the three times
> Has never helped it: it is empty and limpid.
> Into the darkness of drowsiness, dullness, and gloom
> It has never strayed: it is pellucid and clear.
> The eighty thousand deluded thoughts related to the three
> times
> Have never clouded it: it is lucid and awake.
> The multifarious appearances of objects of the eight
> consciousnesses
> Have never obstructed it: it is free and spacious.

Here, where the root text says, "not torpid, ... vivid, unclouded, awake," these are just a few of the plethora of Great Perfection expressions that include pellucid, awake, vivid, naked, peaceful, pure, and hazy.[43] Such words are the inexpressible resonance, the outer manifestation and display, of the Great Perfection, like the spontaneous roar of a lion. They are used at present as a code to guide us on the path. One will not find them explained in terms that intellectuals use. Rather, they are the vocalizations of practitioners who have seen their true nature and rest in that state. They are based on their experience and have specific implications. They are also very helpful for one's practice. This explanation was an oral teaching by my sublime teacher.

In brief, this clear, vivid awareness, the fourth state in which the other three are absent, as explained above, is groundless and rootless, an objectless, open, unimpeded display, in which conceptual elaborations such as birth and cessation are entirely absent. It does not tend to one side or the other—existence or nonexistence, both or neither, exclusion or inclusion, and so on. It is free of extremes such as permanence and discontinuity. It is "unlimited in extent," meaning that it does not tend to a particular size. It is beyond the realm of coming and going—going somewhere or coming from somewhere. And it is the primordial wisdom that pervades the whole of samsara and nirvana. Langdro Könchok Jungne[44] speaks of it as follows:

> There is within the mind
> An inconceivable experience,
> Naked, self-illuminating.
> It embraces all samsara and nirvana.
> It is the wisdom mind of the victorious ones
> Past, present, and to come.

This primordial wisdom pervading the whole of samsara and nirvana is neither one nor various, for as it is said,

> It is not single, for it knows and illuminates the many.
> It is not many, for it is indivisible, a single, same taste.

This awareness that is the fourth state in which the three are absent is devoid of conceptual grasping and notions such as, "It is this; it is not that." As it is said,

> It is beyond thoughts or words, "It is this; it is not that."
> It is free of all conceptual distinctions as good or bad.

Accordingly, it is the great freedom from mental elaborations, awareness that no analogies or words can indicate. Nevertheless, if one were to try and indicate it using a conventional analogy, it is like the clear sky, unobscured by dust, wind, and clouds—pure primordial wisdom, where the contaminants of conceptual constructs and fixation have dissolved into the ultimate expanse. And it has three distinctive features: its nature is emptiness, yet its own character manifests in the form of luminosity, and its cognizant power is open and unobstructed.

e) Introducing the Great Natural Openness and Freedom of Awareness That Is Free of All Assertions

> Ineffable, inconceivable, inexpressible transcendent
>   wisdom,
> Unborn, unceasing, with the true nature of space,
> Open and free by itself, it is the domain of
>   primordial wisdom alone.
> Here, there is no ignorance and no awareness.

This present self-arisen awareness is free of all assertions. Just as it is for a dumb person tasting molasses, no words can describe it. No thought can conceive it, for it is devoid of all deluded concepts related to the three times, like the sky free of clouds. No language made up of words can be used to express it. This indescribable, open and unimpeded awareness is referred to as "transcendent wisdom." From the very beginning it has never been born: it is empty like the expanse of space, beyond the attributes of a subject or object that is born. And yet its appearance aspect manifests unceasingly, as clearly as the stars and planets in the sky. In *The Precious Treasury of the Fundamental Nature* we read,

> When objects appearing unceasingly and brightly
> Like the stars and planets
> Are not adulterated by being evaluated,
> One has now arrived at the level of the highest wisdom,
> Nonconceptual, self-cognizing awareness.[45]

Thus, although its nature is unborn, its inherent radiance is unobstructed. The true mode of being of self-cognizing awareness is like space. When one settles in meditative equipoise in this state, any defilements and other thoughts that may arise naturally subside

in the space of awareness like the knot in a snake undoing itself
and like snow falling on hot rock. This great self-subsiding upon
self-arising is the method for preserving self-cognizing primordial
wisdom.

When one preserves self-cognizing primordial wisdom in this
way, awareness—empty, luminous, and inexpressible—is laid bare.
This is the domain of primordial wisdom alone. It is not at all the
domain of dualistic conceptual thoughts. If one practices like this,
at some point one will realize self-cognizing primordial awareness
and master one's skill in this. At that time, as when on an island
of precious gold, even if one looks, one will never find ordinary
stones, whatever manifests does so as the display of great primordial wisdom. Here, there is nothing to reject—so-called ignorance
and defilements, the three poisons and five poisons—because the
five poisons have been transformed into the five wisdoms. And,
in the absence of ignorance, there is nothing to adopt either—no
fixation on so-called awareness being the opposite of ignorance.
As it is said,

> Since all is awareness, there is no ignorance.
> In the absence of ignorance, there is no deviation from
>   awareness
> And hence no concept of something that deviates.

f) Introducing the Great Equality of Awareness, Appearance and Emptiness Inseparable

> All the phenomena that appear dualistically as
>   samsara and nirvana
> Have no existence as perceived objects and
>   perceiving subjects.
> From the moment they appear, they are empty by
>   nature;
> And while they are empty, by nature they appear.

There is only equality—appearance and emptiness
   inseparable.
If there is no agent equalizing them as being
   inseparable,
Neither can there be the act of equalizing in
   equality.
This primordial wisdom, the luminosity deep
   within,
Which is beyond the "state of equality,"
Is the dharmakāya, Samantabhadra's wisdom mind.

All the phenomena that appear as the duo of samsaric existence
and nirvanic peace—the six sense objects that manifest as perceived objects and the six consciousnesses (those of the five senses
and the mind consciousness) that make up the perceiving subject—
are confused as objects and subjects of apprehension, and as a
result we wander continuously in samsara. Yet in the ultimate way
things are, both object and subject have, from the very beginning,
never existed. They have never been born. They have never been
produced. They are groundless, by nature empty. One needs to be
quite convinced of this.

   Nevertheless, although these apparent phenomena do not, in
truth, exist, we might think that when they appear to our present
deluded perceptions, they do exist. This is not the case. Even while
appearing to our present deluded perceptions, they have never
existed. They do not exist in any way; they are by nature empty, as
is stated in *The Precious Treasury of the Fundamental Nature*:

   Phenomenal existence, samsara and nirvana,
   All things appearing in awareness,
   In the moment of their being perceived,
   Have but the nature of emptiness alone.
   They are like magical illusions, dreams,
   Like moons reflected in the water.

[Wholly empty and primordially empty,
Beyond conceptual elaboration,][46]
They dwell within awareness
Space-like, insubstantial,
The ground of their appearance.[47]

Not only do these appearing phenomena not exist ultimately, but even as they appear and manifest now, they have no existence: they are by nature empty. In *The Precious Treasury of the Dharmadhātu*, we find,

A various display arises naturally:
Phenomenal existence, samsara and nirvana.
In their moment of arising,
Things are by their nature empty forms.
Because they are unborn, they appear to be born.
Yet in their moment of appearing,
There is nothing that is born.[48]

When we say that all the phenomena of samsara and nirvana are empty, we are not saying that their emptiness is a void nothingness, that they are like the horn of a rabbit. Rather, despite their being empty, they are present in the form of the natural luminosity that is the character of emptiness. Although they are empty, by nature they appear; their appearance is unobstructedly present, like the reflection of the moon appearing on a lake. Thus, while they appear, they are empty; and while they are empty, they appear. Their appearance does not stop their being empty, and their emptiness does not impede their appearance. One needs to understand that appearance and emptiness coincide or that they are inseparable, a sole state of equality.

So it is that while appearing phenomena do not exist, they manifest in all kinds of ways; and while emptiness does not exist as such, it pervades everything. As Longchenpa says,

Though nonexistent when appearing,
Phenomena arise in all their various forms.
Though nonexistent in their emptiness,
Things are present everywhere.[49]

In fact, these apparent phenomena are neither appearance nor are
they emptiness, nor are they both appearance and emptiness, and
they are definitely not neither. There is not even an agent equalizing them as being inseparable. In the *Unwritten Tantra* it is said,

It is not appearance, neither does it make things appear.
It is not empty, nor does it exist as emptiness.
It is not luminosity, and there is no concept of luminosity.
It has not moved, is not moving, and will not move.

And *The Precious Treasury of the Dharmadhātu* says,

[The nature of the all-encompassing enlightened mind]
Is not appearance; it transcends appearing things.
It is not emptiness, for it transcends all empty things.
It is not existent; it has no substance and no properties.
It is not nonexistent; it pervades samsara and nirvana.
Not existent and not nonexistent; present of itself and even,
It is the vast primordial expanse.[50]

In this way, all appearances are equalized in the great equality
free of the four extremes; yet even this equality cannot be seen
to exist truly for it is beyond all assertions, free of all conceptual
elaborations. Therefore, this state of equality is beyond categor-
ical assertions such as "This is a state of equality." It is the mind
of all the buddhas of the three times inseparable from the great
dharmadhātu, awareness that is luminous deep within. This
great primordial wisdom is the wisdom mind of the dharmakāya
Samantabhadra.

2) Showing the Means for Making Awareness Manifest

This section is divided into five parts: (1) showing how it is made manifest when one settles naturally in the state devoid of something to be seen and someone who sees; (2) explaining how, if one relies on effortful meditation practice, one will not see the fundamental nature beyond meditation; (3) how the way of being of samsara and nirvana becomes manifest clearly and distinctly; (4) distilling all the appearances of samsara and nirvana into the single, primordially pure awareness; and (5) showing that all the phenomena of samsara and nirvana are of one taste in awareness, the state of the great equality.

a) Showing How Awareness Is Made Manifest When One Settles Naturally in the State Devoid of Something to Be Seen and Someone Who Sees

> Potentially either buddha or sentient being,
> Mind in its immediate nowness, fresh,
>   unadulterated,
> Unobscured, clear and pure in every part—
> When one looks at it, one cannot see it;
> When one leaves it be, one sees.
> From the beginning there has never been
> Any deliberate "seeing" of it.

If one realizes the dharmakāya, the fundamental nature of awareness that is present as the ground, just as it is, and experiences it through practice, one will be freed as a buddha. If one fails to recognize it and is overpowered by the clinging to a self, one will be deluded as a sentient being. It is because of this difference between recognizing awareness and failing to recognize it that there can be either nirvana or samsara. This fundamental nature is mind in its immediate nowness, the fresh state of awareness unchanged by circumstances and unadulterated by clinging, the naked awareness aspect of unimpeded emptiness-luminosity. There is not as much as a hair's worth of contamination by deluded thoughts related to past, present, and future. Since it is not obscured, it is open and unimpeded. It is clear and pure in every part, inside and out, at the periphery and at the center, like the perfectly clear sky. This is the essence of the wisdom mind of all the buddhas, the sovereign view known throughout samsara and nirvana as the Great Perfection.

Should fortunate persons with a karmic connection who want to encounter the true nature of that state directly look at it as if there were something to be looked at and someone looking at it, they will not see anything. But if they let their body, speech, and mind rest naturally, without contrivance, and settle in a state of relaxation without there being anything to look at, they will see the true nature of awareness, the state of limpid clarity and emptiness. This can be illustrated by an analogy. If one wishes to see the reflection of the moon in clear water and one stirs the water with a stick, it will become troubled and one will not see what one is looking for. However, if one leaves the water to settle without shaking, stirring, or churning it, and then look, one will see the moon's white reflection shining brightly. In *The Cloudless Sky*,[51] we read,

> When, for example, water in a vessel is mixed with dirt,
> One may shake or stir or churn it, but despite a hundred
>   efforts,
> The water will never clear—it will be a mass of dirt.
> Leave it as it is, and it will become clear on its own.
> Likewise, one will never find ultimate reality, the essence of
>   the sugatas,
> By looking for it: however much one tries, one will not see it.
> Completely let go of the activities of body, speech, and
>   mind.
> Relax in your fundamental condition, and it will naturally
>   manifest.

Where the root text says, "From the beginning there has never been any deliberate 'seeing' of it," it means that when one is fettered by conceptual fixation, thinking "This is seeing the true nature of awareness," and one is influenced by faults that corrupt one's practice, such as efforts to repress some things and achieve others, one is unable to see the true nature of awareness.

b) Explaining How, If One Relies on Effortful Meditation Practice, One Will Not See the Fundamental Nature beyond Meditation

> It transcends anything to be attained through meditation.
> In this respect, fools fetter themselves:
> They talk about accomplishing buddhahood
> And look outside and practice energetically.
> Although those who practice are [already] buddhas,
> They search elsewhere,
> And thinking that the buddha cannot be within
>   themselves,
> They become depressed.
> From the buddha, their own awareness,
> They will be cut off for a long time.

When one is meditating by preserving the true nature of awareness, as explained above, if one meditates with the idea that there is a subject and object, a meditator and something to meditate on, one will fall prey to concepts that the three spheres[52] exist truly. Consequently, it will be impossible to realize what it means to be rid of a "meditation" mentality, for as Dudjom Lingpa says,

> There is no reflection, no meditation, no preserving, no nurturing, no distraction.

Thus, the highest of all meditations is to preserve the state of non-meditation, devoid of meditation and meditator. The result too is but the four kāyas and five primordial wisdoms present in oneself. There is no aspiration for a result that is to be attained from elsewhere. It is the "result of the Great Perfection beyond attainment," transcending anything to be attained through meditation. Fools who fail to understand this hold views with conceptual references, their meditation involves rejection and adoption, their conduct involves dualistic grasping, and their result is full of expectation and apprehension. They are fettering themselves. Failing to recognize that buddha—that is, awareness—is present within themselves, they talk about accomplishing buddhahood, and looking outward, or thinking that buddhahood exists elsewhere and that it manifests in a beautiful form with the major and minor marks, they put a lot of effort into practicing to attain that state. In so doing, they are making the mistake of taking the wrong path, as is stated in the *Diamond Cutter Sūtra*:

> Those who see me as physical form,
> Who perceive me as sound,
> Have entered the wrong path.
> Such people are not seeing me.

Such practitioners, trying to attain buddhahood, fail to recognize that awareness is buddha. Instead, it seems to them that "buddha" has gone to another realm and that they will have to look for him. They think that buddhahood cannot be within themselves, and so they lose heart. Among Shabkar's writings, we find,

> That which we call "buddha," the sound of whose name
> Resonates like thunder throughout samsara and nirvana,
> Is eternally present in the mindstreams of sentient beings in
> the six realms,
> Accompanying them, without for an instant abandoning
> them—how marvelous!

And,

> How strange that people do not know that buddha is
>   present within themselves
> And that they look for buddha somewhere else.
> How strange that, though it is clearly manifest, like the
>   brightly shining heart of the sun,
> There are so few who are able to see it.

People who hold that buddha is elsewhere are cut off from the true nature of the buddha, their own awareness, for a long time and are unable to encounter it.

c) How the Way of Being of Samsara and Nirvana Becomes Manifest Clearly and Distinctly

> **When the sun of self-cognizing awareness, the**
> **   dharmakāya, rises,**
> **The way of abiding, above, of Samantabhadra;**
> **The mode of existence, below, of the hell beings in**
> **   Torment Unsurpassed;**
> **The causes (virtue and evil) and their ripened**
> **   results, together with their root;**
> **The system of the two truths;**
> **Ground, path, and result, and so on;**
> **Subject and object—all these, with nothing mixed,**
> **Are seen with the great primordial wisdom,**
> **Distinctly, as they are.**

After the self-arisen, self-cognizing awareness has been recognized, clearly and distinctly, one preserves that state through meditation, and there comes a point when one has perfected one's skill in this and the wisdom that knows the true nature of phenomena and that which knows all phenomena in their multiplicity become manifest. The sun of self-cognizing awareness, the dharmakāya, has risen. At that time, with the primordial wisdom that realizes the true nature of phenomena, one understands the profound fundamental nature of all the phenomena in samsara and nirvana just as it is. And with the primordial wisdom that sees all phenomena in their multiplicity, one clearly perceives the way of abiding, above, of Primordial Lord Samantabhadra; the mode of existence, below, of the beings in the eighteen hells down to the hell of Torment Unsurpassed, who are experiencing the sufferings due to their karmic perceptions; and the individual experiences of happiness and suffering in the six realms, which are the ripened results of the multifarious causes (virtuous and evil deeds) together with their root that the beings there have accumulated. Furthermore, the system of the two truths and all the inconceivable categories of phenomena such as ground, path, and fruit, subject and object, and so on appear just as they are, individually clear and distinct, like a face in a mirror, perceived with the great primordial wisdom that sees distinctly all phenomena in their multiplicity.

Awareness and the primordial wisdom that knows the nature and multiplicity of phenomena and manifests from the creative power and display of awareness are inseparable, like the sun and its rays. This is a special quality of the great awareness-dharmakāya.

d) Distilling All the Appearances of Samsara and Nirvana into the Single, Primordially Pure Awareness

> Though the appearing objects of the six
>   consciousnesses manifest unceasingly,
> They unfold as the creative power and display of
>   awareness.
> The multifarious appearances of samsara and
>   nirvana,
> Good and bad, pleasure and pain and their causes,
> And subject and object all constitute a single
>   expanse,
> A single taste, a single state of evenness.

Even though the appearing objects of the six sense consciousnesses

(form, sound, smell, taste, physical sensations, and pain and pleasure, and so forth, which are the objects respectively of the eyes,
ears, nose, tongue, body, and mind) manifest unceasingly and vividly, they are not manifesting as something other than or separate
from awareness. Rather, they unfold as the creative power and display of the great self-cognizing primordial awareness. Thus they
have the same essence as awareness, the same taste and the same
nature. Omniscient Longchenpa explains,

> The one awareness is the ground of all phenomena.
> However many they may seem,
> They do not waver from their one sole nature.
> So it is said. Their one and only root
> Is primal wisdom self-arisen.[53]

Likewise, even though the appearances of samsara and nirvana,
evil and good, and the appearances of happiness and suffering and
their causes, and the appearances of subject and object appear as
they do, since all of these multifarious appearances are the creative
power and display of awareness, they are of the same nature, the
same expanse, the same taste, as awareness. *The Precious Treasury
of the Fundamental Nature* explains it thus:

> In certain situations from a single gem,
> Fire and water, different and distinct, may both emerge.
> And yet their root is one, the pure and precious lapis lazuli.
> Likewise even though from one awareness self-cognizing,
> Nirvana and samsara both arise,
> Their root is one, the ultimate enlightened mind.[54]

All the pure and impure appearances that seem to be separate from
awareness are thus established as being of the same nature as awareness. They are a state of vast evenness. This is a sublime key point.

e) Showing That All the Phenomena of Samsara and Nirvana Are of One Taste in Awareness, the State of the Great Equality

> Appearances are equal, arisings are equal,
> Empty phenomena are equal, non-empty
>   phenomena are equal,
> Space is equal, everything is equal—
> The all-pervading expanse of equality.
> Like the reflections in the ocean (which is never
>   changed by circumstances)
> Of the stars and planets shining in the firmament,
> Phenomena manifest clearly and distinctly
> In the expanse of the great space [of awareness].
> Samsara and nirvana are equal,
> Encompassed by the expanse of Samantabhadra.
> Sustained calm and profound insight are
>   inseparable,
> One taste, the indescribable, inexpressible,
> Uncontrived state beyond ordinary mind.
> To recognize this nature is the view.

The things that appear now during the day in the form of apprehended objects such as the mountains, rocks, and houses of the outer world, and the appearances of the world and its inhabitants that appeared last night in the form of apprehended objects in a dream—both are equal in the primordially pure expanse of awareness. The consciousness that arises as the apprehending mind now during the day and the consciousness that manifests as the apprehending mind during one's dreams are also both equal in the primordially pure expanse of awareness. Similarly, the empty ultimate truth and the appearing relative truth are both equal in the primordially pure expanse of awareness. Moreover, appearances such as pillars and pots that are considered to be truly [existent and] not empty and appearances that are held to be truly empty are also both equal in the primordially pure expanse of awareness. Things like space that appear insubstantial and things like one's body and possessions that appear and are held to be substantial are also both equal in the primordially pure expanse of awareness.

In short, everything—good or bad, pleasurable or painful, wholesome or unwholesome—is of one taste in awareness, the all-pervading expanse of equality. There is not a single thing that is not equal in the all-pervading expanse of equality, as the Great Omniscient One points out:

> Things and nonthings are equal in the ultimate expanse.
> Buddhas and beings are equal in the ultimate expanse.
> The relative and ultimate are equal in the ultimate expanse.
> Defects and good qualities are equal in the ultimate expanse.
> Main and secondary directions, zenith, nadir—
> All are equal in the ultimate expanse.[55]

And in the same text he says,

> Without objective reference or interruption,
> It is the expanse of equality.
> The nature of all things is dharmatā, equality itself.
> Thus not a single thing but rests in that equality!
> In this one equality are all things equal—
> Such is the condition of the enlightened mind.[56]

In like manner, just as the ocean is unchanged by circumstances and is always without movement, none of the phenomena of samsara and nirvana ever move from awareness, the sphere of great equality. While all the reflections of the planets and stars shining in the sky appear clearly and vividly in the ocean, those reflections are not separate from it but are equal with it. Similarly, while all phenomena arise by themselves clearly and distinctly in the sphere of awareness, the great expanse of equality, samsara and nirvana are encompassed equally by the expanse of the dharmakāya, Samanta-bhadra, with nothing being kept or removed. As Longchenpa says,

Constantly within the great expanse,
Awareness self-cognizing,
All arises equal and as equal dwells.
All is equal in subsiding, neither good nor bad.
There's nothing that's not equal to awareness,
Nothing that does not abide,
And nothing that does not subside therein.
All things are essentialized
As being the immense primordial expanse
Of the enlightened state.[57]

Similarly, sustained calm, in which the mind is completely still, and profound insight, in which one vividly knows or clearly sees the fundamental nature of the mind, pervade and are both of one taste in awareness, the great equality that is the inexpressible inseparability of emptiness and luminosity. There is no higher view than that. And the fundamental nature of such a view is the true uncontrived state, indescribable, inexpressible, beyond the ordinary mind. To recognize this nature is the authentic view.

ii. How to Preserve the True Nature of Awareness by Practicing the Path of Nonmeditation

When one encounters the true nature of self-
cognizing awareness, Samantabhadra,
There is no meditation separate from it.
Through its mere recognition, [thoughts] subside therein.
Apart from that, to fixate on meditation is to
obscure the nature of awareness.
By resting without looking, one will instantly
encounter its true nature.
Nonmeditation is the meditation on the natural
openness and freedom of the mind.

When one realizes the self-cognizing awareness that is the

inseparability of sustained calm and profound insight (as explained above)—in other words, the naked awareness, empty, luminous, and unceasing—one encounters in reality the true nature of the dharmakāya Samantabhadra. At that time, it is important to preserve that state by means of meditation. And when one is meditating, what we call "meditation" is not some separate meditation that is different from and other than the view. As Patrul Rinpoche says,

> In short, recognizing one's own nature is the view.
> Remaining in that state is the meditation.
> Integrating that with circumstances is the key point of the
> conduct.
> To make no distinction between view, meditation, and
> conduct is most important.

Accordingly, other than never straying from the view, there is no meditation involving something to meditate on and someone meditating, as is explained in *Mirror of Samantabhadra's Mind*:

> The view is uncontrived—the open and unimpeded state of
> primordial wisdom.
> The meditation is uncontrived—there is no grasping at
> clarity.
> The conduct is uncontrived—spontaneous and relaxed.
> The result is uncontrived—the state of self-arisen awareness.

As it is said, view, meditation, conduct, and result are all necessarily set forth as a single awareness. Simply recognizing the nature of awareness, one should not reject or indulge in any thoughts that arise, or repress some and encourage others. When one preserves the true nature of awareness in this way, in the state of awareness itself thoughts manifest by themselves and subside by themselves, like drawings on water. This is how to preserve the state of awareness through meditation. On the other hand, if one fixates on something to meditate on and someone meditating, one will be obscuring the nature of awareness, and one's meditation will go the wrong way. So without looking, as if there were something to look at and someone looking, one should rest naturally without contrivance, and in an instant one will encounter the true nature of awareness, as clear and bright as the sky free of the three blemishes.[58]

Nonmeditation transcends meditation. If one recognizes the fundamental nature, this is the meditation on the natural openness and freedom of the mind itself. As Shabkar says,

> Nonmeditation transcends meditation. Meditation brings ruin.
> What cannot be observed transcends view. What is there to view?

The view, meditation, conduct, and result are all necessarily incorporated into the sole state of awareness. Patrul Rinpoche says,

> What is the view? It is the important point of being without clinging.
> What is the meditation? It is the key point of being without grasping.
> What is the conduct? The best is that which accords with the teachings.
> It is vital to bring view, meditation, and conduct all together.

And Mipham Rinpoche declares,

> The view is without clinging and inherently clear.
> The meditation is groundless and without root.
> The conduct is a happy mind free of bias.
> The result is natural openness and freedom, the three kāyas.

It is important to understand this—that view, meditation, conduct, and result are all nothing other than a single awareness.

iii. An Explanation of the Conduct That Accords with the Natural Openness and Freedom of the Mind and Accompanies the View and Meditation

There are two parts: (1) the main teaching on the conduct that accords with the natural openness and freedom of the mind and (2) a supplementary explanation on avoiding the dangers of deviating, straying, and erring.

A) The Main Teaching on the Conduct That Accords with the Natural Openness and Freedom of the Mind

> When one has gained stability,
> Without any distinction between meditation and
> postmeditation,
> Good conduct brings no benefit,
> Nor does bad conduct constitute a fault.
> Good and bad thoughts, like waves on water,
> Subside in four ways in the state of great natural
> openness and freedom;
> Like the rays of the sun, they subside by themselves.
> This is the conduct that accords
> With the natural openness and freedom of the mind.

When, through meditation, one preserves the fundamental state of the view, it is important to maintain a balance between being too concentrated and too relaxed, with no distinction between formal meditation and postmeditation. Machik Labdrön says,

> Be firmly concentrated and loosely relaxed:
> Here is a key point for the view.

By preserving the view in this way, one should gradually achieve the experiences of movement, attainment, familiarity, stability, and perfection.[59] At some point, one will achieve stability, and when that happens, one can truly follow the yogic way of conduct in which one experiences everything as having the same taste. At this stage, on the level of ultimate reality, virtuous activities will bring no benefit. If one has realized the meaning of the great primordial purity, which has been pure from the very beginning, good conduct consisting of virtuous activities such as prostrations, circumambulations, and the purification of obscurations brings no benefit. By the same token, once one has realized awareness, the great purity and equality of phenomenal existence, there is not even an atom's worth to be seen of impurities such as deluded actions and habitual tendencies, so that bad conduct similarly does not constitute a fault. Even activities that are associated with attachment, aversion, or bewilderment, for example, do no harm. Rather, the five poisons subside; they are open and free as the five primordial wisdoms. At that time, it does not matter whether good or bad thoughts manifest. They manifest by themselves and subside by themselves, like waves on water. Consequently, all one's activities, good or bad, are ornaments of the great, naturally open and free awareness. Then, everything that manifests subsides (that is, it is open and free) in four ways—namely, open and free from the beginning, open and free from extremes, naturally open and free, and directly open and free. There is not a single phenomenon that is not open and free. Moreover, since everything that arises manifests by itself and subsides by itself, it is the state of the great naturally open and free awareness. It subsides by itself like the rays of the sun. The fundamental state is realized. This is what we call "the conduct that accords with the natural openness and freedom of the mind."

Regarding what we said above about there being no difference between good and bad conduct, although there are intrepid practitioners who actually follow the yogic way of conduct in which one experiences everything as having the same taste, people like us cannot compare to them. The great beings of the past said,

> One should be daring in one's view,
> But one's conduct must be finely honed.

And the Great Oḍḍiyāna said,

> One's view should be higher than the sky,
> But one's attention to actions and their effects should be
> finer than flour.

These are instructions for people like us. In similar vein, Dudjom Lingpa advises,

> One's conduct must not slip toward the view:
> One should be like someone coming before the king to be
> judged.
> Nor should one's view slip toward conduct:
> One should be like a lion guarding a snowy mountain.

Until we reach the level of the exhaustion of phenomena in dharmatā, fire will still feel hot to the touch and water will still feel cold. So it is very important for people like us to perform as many positive, virtuous deeds as we can, to do our best to avoid even the smallest negative, unvirtuous deeds, and especially to have confidence in the karmic law of cause and effect, develop faith and devotion, and train in compassion for sentient beings. On the other hand, to pretend that we have a little bit of the view and to conduct ourselves perversely is absolutely wrong. The Omniscient Teacher says,

> So never say that there's no cause and no effect.
> Conditioned things dependently arise,
> Are inconceivable, past numbering.
> The hallucinations of samsara, and even states
> Of peace and bliss are countless and beyond the mind's
> imagining.
> All dependently arise from the gathering of causes and
> conditions.[60]

One must be quite certain in one's mind as to the significance of this.

B) A Supplementary Explanation on Avoiding the Dangers of Deviations, Errors, and Mistakes

> Whatever meditative experiences, good or bad,
>   occur—
> Experiences of bliss, luminosity,
> Absence of thought, and so on that one might
>   cling to—
> One should not do anything to encourage good ones
> Or counteract bad ones;
> One should leave them be, free of grasping.
> When one settles, free of contrivance and without
>   fixation,
> They subside by themselves in the natural state.
> The many kinds of deviations, errors, and mistakes
>   can then never occur.

When, as explained above, the view has been recognized and one preserves that state in meditation, various predictable and unpredictable experiences may occur as one's meditation waxes or wanes. For example, one may have meditative experiences, with or without clinging, of bliss like the warmth of a fire, luminosity like the breaking of the day, or absence of thought like a lake undisturbed by waves. When these occur, one must be sure to destroy experiences that are accompanied by clinging. As it is said,

> The more the yogi is destroying the meditation, the better
>   it is.
> The stronger the water falls, the better it is.

Otherwise, if one clings to experiences of bliss, luminosity, and absence of thought, being sidetracked by bliss will project one into the world of desire, being sidetracked by clarity will project one into the world of form, and being sidetracked by absence of thought will project one into the formless world.

If one has the capacity to meditate with great endeavor and determination, all sorts of good and bad experiences will occur. Mipham says,

> From time without beginning, all sorts of habitual thoughts and waves of karmic wind have occurred, unpredictably and without measure. It has been like someone setting out on a long journey and seeing places with all sorts of troubles. So we have to preserve our own path without fixating on whatever manifests. In particular, while we are still not used to this, when we have the experience of movement, with all sorts of thoughts flaring up like a fire, we must not let it worry us. If we can preserve [the meditation], without relinquishing the right balance between concentration and relaxation, the subsequent experiences of attainment and so on will gradually occur.

There is a common saying:

> There is nothing that does not come up in a yogi's experience;
> There is nothing that does not grow on summer pasture.

Accordingly, when one is able to preserve the flow of the practice, many different experiences can occur—blissful experiences, troubling experiences, experiences of absence of thought, limpidity, ugliness, and clarity, experiences of clinging and absence of clinging, experiences with grasping and without grasping, pleasant and unpleasant experiences, and so on. But whatever experiences occur, without doing anything to encourage good experiences or counteract bad ones, one should leave them be without grasping at them.

In this way, whatever experiences manifest, one should settle without contrivance in the state of awareness. Without rejecting or adopting anything, or trying to block or accomplish anything, without expectation or apprehension, without fixation, one should maintain one's own natural state, the great equality, awareness free of elaboration. Experiences will then arise by themselves and subside by themselves, like a knot in a snake undoing itself, snow falling on hot rock, or a thief entering an empty house—they will not affect one's meditation in any way, beneficially or adversely. At that time, there will be no danger of one's falling prey to the many different kinds of deviations, errors, and mistakes.

iv. How the Twenty-Five Aspects of the Result Are Inherently Complete in Awareness

> As for the twenty-five aspects of the ultimate result
>   that are obtained,
> The five kāyas are the dharmakāya, saṃbhogakāya,
>   nirmāṇakāya,
> Unchanging vajrakāya, and the abhisaṃbodhikāya.
> The five kinds of enlightened speech are the
>   ultimate, unborn speech;
> That which transmits the buddhas' wisdom through
>   symbols;
> Expression through words; the inseparable vajra
>   speech;
> And the speech of enlightenment, awareness.
> The five kinds of enlightened mind are the wisdom
>   of the dharmadhātu,
> Mirrorlike wisdom, the wisdom of equality,
> All-perceiving wisdom, and all-accomplishing
>   wisdom.
> The five enlightened qualities are the buddha fields,
> Measureless palaces, rays of light, thrones,
> And ornaments of enjoyment.
> Pacification, increase, gathering under power,
>   wrathful subjugation,
> And spontaneous deeds are the five enlightened
>   activities.

These aspects of the results are not elsewhere—
They are complete in one's own nature
And truly obtained on the level of Mighty Vajradhara.
This is the teaching on the ground of trekchö,
The stage that combines view and conduct.
It is entrusted to fortunate disciples. Sealed!

Having realized that the view, meditation, and conduct are inseparable in the single self-cognizing primordial wisdom and trained in it to perfection, there comes a time when one attains buddhahood in the expanse of the ground of freedom of dharmakāya Samantabhadra, or the ground of freedom of all the buddhas, thereby obtaining the twenty-five aspects of the ultimate result. Of these, first there are the five kāyas.[61]

Once one has perfected the training in this life, awareness that is the ultimate nature, the object of meditation, is blended inseparably with awareness that is cognizant potency, the meditating subject, and freedom is attained in the dharmakāya. Within the state of the dharmakāya, but without moving from it, there appears to pure disciples—that is, bodhisattvas on the ten levels—an untainted body of light, with the major and minor marks. This is the sambhogakāya. And to impure disciples—beings in the six realms—there appears in accordance with beings' characters, faculties, and aspirations the nirmāṇakāya that acts for the benefit of beings: the animate nirmāṇakāya, the nirmāṇakāya that manifests as art and artists, the diversified nirmāṇakāya, and so forth. Although, while never moving from the dharmakāya, the sambhogakāya and nirmāṇakāya appear as the two rūpakāyas, ultimately the dharmakāya and rūpakāya are inseparable. This inseparability is the unchanging vajrakāya. All these are spontaneously present as the nature of self-cognizing primordial wisdom, and while never moving from the state of the dharmakāya, they appear in a variety of ways according to the karma of beings to be trained. Their spontaneous presence and multifarious appearance constitute the abhisambodhikāya.[62]

The five kinds of enlightened speech are as follows. The unborn ultimate reality is inexpressible, but from the point of view of its being the ground of all expression, it is the unborn, ultimate speech, related to the dharmakāya. Then, without moving from the state of awareness, its creative power and display appears in the form of nonhumans such as wisdom ḍākinīs to indicate the meaning of the teachings to the disciples' minds by means of symbols. This is the speech related to the saṃbhogakāya that transmits the buddhas' wisdom through symbols. Next there is the speech that is expressed in words, related to the nirmāṇakāya, which appears to beings to be trained, teaching the Dharma simultaneously in accord with their different languages as a way of instructing them according to their specific needs. All languages exist as sound and emptiness indivisible and are thus free from the two extremes: this is the inseparable vajra speech.[63] In the state of awareness all sounds are spontaneously produced and are thus not obstructed in any way. This is the blessed speech of awareness, the speech of manifest enlightenment, making five kinds of enlightened speech in all.

Of the five kinds of enlightened mind, the wisdom of the dharmadhātu corresponds to the mind related to the great absence of thought of the dharmakāya. Mirrorlike wisdom corresponds to the mind related to the clear and complete knowledge of the abhisaṃbodhikāya. The wisdom of equality corresponds to the enlightened mind related to the great equality of the saṃbhogakāya. All-perceiving wisdom corresponds to the indestructible vajra mind. All-accomplishing wisdom corresponds to the mind related to the nirmāṇakāya that liberates beings.

The first of the five enlightened qualities are the buddha fields, as mentioned in a tantra:[64] "Buddha fields in all the ten directions" and "Inconceivable pure realms." Likewise, there are the measureless palaces, which are beyond such concepts as extent and limits, as we read in the same tantra: "The measureless palace beyond extent." Concerning the brilliant, perfectly pure rays of light, the tantra speaks of "great masses of radiating lights." As for the thrones, the tantra mentions, "The most extraordinary thrones are great thrones borne by lions, elephants, horses, peacocks, and garuḍas, on which are a sun, moon, and precious lotus." Finally, there are the ornaments of enjoyment, a wealth of everything delightful: "All kinds of musical offerings, massed like clouds." These are the five enlightened qualities among the aspects of the result.

Of the five enlightened activities, the first is the activity of pacification, which is the activity of removing the entire mass of defilements in the mindstreams of beings to be trained, as is stated in the *Tantra Fragment "Stirring the Depths"*:

> To those whose minds are filled with defiled thoughts,
> The buddhas' deeds bring balance and peace.[65]

Similarly, there is the activity of enriching beings who are poor and increasing their lifespan and merit. The same source has,

> People who are ignorant or poor and destitute
> Are enriched with infinite knowledge and wealth.

The buddhas' activities also gather under their power stubborn, unruly beings, as indicated in the same work:

> People who cannot be helped or disciplined
> Are subdued and pacified by the activity of power.

Evil beings who are hard to tame and cannot be subdued by skillful acts are subjugated by means of wrathful activities and drawn into the expanse in which delusion is unknown. Again, the same tantra says,

> Malevolent beings who cannot be tamed by compassionate
>   means
> Are subjugated by wrathful intervention.

As well as these, there is the activity of spontaneous deeds, which comprises impartial deeds based on kindness and love for unrealized, deluded beings:

Thus, for the different kinds of unrealized beings,
The buddhas act impartially and spontaneously.

These are the five enlightened activities of the buddhas.

The twenty-five aspects of the result are not produced somewhere else; they are spontaneously complete within the nature of awareness, without needing to be striven for. When they become manifest, one has truly attained the level of Mighty Vajradhara.

The text up to here has shown the path that combines the view, meditation, and conduct of the ground of trekchö, or the stage of integrating view, meditation, conduct, and result all into the single primordially pure awareness. Applying the seal of secrecy, the author says, "I entrust it to you, fortunate disciples, children of my heart. Put it into practice!"

b. The Practice of Spontaneous Presence, Thögal—by Which Diligent Persons Gain Freedom through Effort

This section is divided into (1) the main explanation of thögal and (2) supplementary instructions on the four bardos.

i. The Main Explanation of Thögal

The main explanation comprises (1) a brief introduction and (2) a detailed explanation.

A) Brief Introduction

The direct path of spontaneous presence, thögal,
    involving effort,
Is the secret path of luminosity related to the vajra
    chains:

> Through it, hallucinatory appearances (not existing
>   yet appearing to exist)
> Manifest as the untainted kāyas and wisdoms.
> The instructions for manifest buddhahood
> Concern the means for attaining it through the four
>   visions—
> Called the vision of the dharmatā in reality,
> Enhanced experiences of awareness,
> The climax of awareness,
> And the exhaustion of phenomena transcending
>   ordinary mind.

These are the instructions on the profound, direct path of spontaneous presence, thögal, involving effort, through which diligent beings attain freedom by means of strenuous practice. Although the present hallucinatory appearances do not exist, as a result of one's taking them to exist, they are perceived as the outer universe (earth and stones, mountains and rocks) and its inner inhabitants. Through the secret path of luminosity, related to the vajra chains, these appearances are transformed and manifest as the untainted, infinitely pure phenomenal existence—that is, the kāyas, primordial wisdoms, and so forth.

Beings with enduring good karma and the greatest diligence who follow these instructions for attaining manifest enlightenment will, in this life, realize self-cognizing awareness, the wisdom mind of the dharmakāya. Through the four visions of spontaneous presence—namely, the visions of dharmatā in reality, enhanced experiences of awareness, the climax of awareness, and reaching the level of the exhaustion of phenomena in the dharmatā or exhaustion of phenomena transcending ordinary mind—they will attain manifest buddhahood. These visions comprise the profound method for doing so.

B) Detailed Explanation

The detailed explanation is divided into (1) a general explanation and (2) a specific explanation

1) A General Explanation

> From the moment it is first formed,
> One's body, like a house, is the physical support
> In which mind and wisdom are present as what is
>   supported,
> Appearing through the pathway of the visual sense
>   organ.
> Thanks to the four lamps, all the visions manifest
> Like the rays issuing from the sun.
> From the natural, original state of calm
> There arises the path of profound insight, awareness,
>   the vajra chains,
> And thence all luminous appearances without
>   exception manifest.
> Not a single being is there to whom they cannot
>   appear.

To introduce this, I will give a little supplementary explanation on how the fundamental nature is naturally and unceasingly present in the vajra body as the ground for the manifestation of the six lamps. In the beginning, when this vajra body is first formed in one's mother's womb, the channels in the chakra of manifestation in the navel take form, and in the navel the impure eyes of the elements and the refined eyes of wisdom, which are just two dots similar to fish eyes, are formed together. Then, thanks to these, the chakras in the heart, throat, crown, and secret centers are formed one by one. The central channel and *roma* and *kyangma* are formed from the navel center as the life tree traversing the middle of the five chakras. The impure eyes of the elements give rise to the impure channels, winds, and essence-drops. Within the pupils, the essence of the visual organ, there arise the physical sense organs that enable one to see forms. They apprehend the impure appearances of deluded perceptions but do not see the pure appearances of primordial wisdom. The refined eyes of wisdom or eyes of the lamp give rise to the pure channels, winds, and essence-drops. The extremely pure light channel does not apprehend the impure hallucinatory appearances but apprehends the pure appearances of primordial wisdom. This, then, is the path that enables one to directly perceive the appearances of luminous ultimate reality. Thus, as one of these two channels (the pure and impure) is stretched out, the other is drawn in.[66]

So, from the beginning when one's own body is formed, it is the physical support, like a house, in which we dwell. Whatever pure or impure appearances manifest do so with the support of this body. The body itself is the support for the mind that is supported and that apprehends pure and impure appearances. All the impure phenomena of the mind and pure phenomena of primordial wisdom appear through the pathway of the two doors of the eyes. Thanks to the four lamps, all the pure appearances of the ultimate expanse, empty disks of light, awareness, and so on manifest unobstructedly like the rays issuing forth from the sun.

Generally speaking, the nature of the mind is originally peaceful. This sustained calm acts as the base from which there arises the profound insight that clearly and nakedly sees the empty, luminous, and unceasing awareness. And through the path of the vajra chains of awareness, there arise all the appearances without exception of the ultimate expanse, empty disks, and awareness. There is not a single sentient being among those who practice this path to whom they cannot appear, for as it is said,

> The essence of the sugatas pervades the totality of beings.

And,

> Even leeches are the stuff of buddhahood.

The essence of the sugatas, awareness, pervades the whole of sentient beings in the same way as oil pervades sesame seeds.

2) A Specific Explanation of the Different Divisions of Thögal

The specific explanation is divided into three sections: (1) how, relying on skillful means, the four lamps are made manifest; (2) how one progresses through the four visions of thögal; and (3) four supporting pith instructions. The first of these is further made up of five parts: (1) how one relinquishes the nine activities of the three doors, (2) relying on four crucial points as the method for making manifest the four lamps, (3) how the visions of the four lamps arise as cause and result, (4) how the four lamps make it possible for the luminous appearances to unfold, and (5) the main explanation of the four lamps.

a) How, Relying on Skillful Means, the Four Lamps Are Made Manifest
i) How One Relinquishes the Nine Activities of the Three Doors

> First, the nine activities of the three doors must be
> relinquished.

Before training in thögal, one must begin by relinquishing the nine activities of the three doors. Physically, this means that one should give up activities on the outer level such as getting the better of one's enemies, caring for one's relatives, and working in business or agriculture. One should relinquish activities on the inner level such as those associated with faith and compassion. And one should cease activities on the secret level such as ritual dances and mudrās. Having done so, one should stay alone, like a wounded wild animal.

Verbally, on the outer level, one should avoid all kinds of deluded conversation; on the inner level, give up the recitations of the approach and accomplishment practices; and on the secret level, cease the recitations related to the channels and winds, and so on. One should remain silent, like the sound of an echo that has died away.

Mentally, one should abandon, on the outer level, all kinds of deluded thoughts; on the inner level, faith and compassion; and on the secret level, the concentrations of the generation and perfection stages, and so on. One should remain in a thoughtless state, like a pool whose inflow is blocked. This is how one should relinquish the nine activities of the three doors.

ii) Relying on Four Crucial Points as the Method for Making Manifest the Four Lamps

> It is in dependence on four key points that the four lamps appear.
> The key point for the body
> Refers to the dharmakāya, saṃbhogakāya, and nirmāṇakāya postures:
> Staying like a lion, elephant, or rishi.
> The key point for the sense door is the gaze,
> With the eyes turned up, cast down, or looking sideways.
> The key point for the speech
> Is to train in breathing gently in and out.
> The key point for the mind
> Is to settle in a state devoid of thoughts of any kind.

To make manifest the four lamps, it is necessary to take support of four key points—the key points related to the body, the sense door, the speech, and the mind. It is by doing so that the appearances of the four lamps manifest. These points thus constitute a profound and sublime method.

First, there is the key point for the body, which refers to the postures of the dharmakāya, saṃbhogakāya, and nirmāṇakāya. These are mentioned in the *Necklace of Pearls Tantra*:

The key point of the body is threefold:
To remain like a lion, an elephant,
Or like a rishi.

The posture of the dharmakāya is like the majestic pose of a lion. The posture of the saṃbhogakāya is like that of a recumbent elephant. The nirmāṇakāya posture is like that of a rishi crouching upright.

The first of these, the majestic pose of a lion, involves squatting with the soles of the feet touching each other, so that the moving wind is pushed down. The body is held straight, so that the wind moves naturally. The neck is turned upward: this is a powerful way to stop thoughts. The fisted hands are planted on the ground inside or outside the thighs: this balances the elements.

Second, the elephant posture involves kneeling with the knees against the chest: this increases the warmth of bliss. The two elbows are placed on the ground, so that the male and female winds are balanced in a genderless state. One's chin rests on the palms of one's hands so that the coarse wind is stopped. The toes are pushed outside the buttocks so as to balance drowsiness and restlessness.

Third, for the rishi posture, one crouches with the body straight to balance the channels and winds. The soles of the feet rest on the ground, suppressing the karmic wind. The spine should be kept straight so that wind and mind move naturally. The arms are crossed round one's knees: this helps to mingle the ultimate expanse and awareness. The ankles should be juxtaposed, joining skillful means and wisdom.

If the pure appearances of primordial wisdom are to manifest, the key point for the body must be respected, by adopting the three postures. Otherwise, the key point for the channels will not be controlled, and without that, the key point of wind and awareness will not be mastered, with the result that the appearances of primordial wisdom will fail to manifest. Therefore, since the [lamp of the utterly pure] expanse and [the lamp of the empty] disks of light pervade the channels of the body, if one does not apply the key points for the body—that is, those of the three postures—they will not manifest. Just as a snake's belly scales are invisible unless one twists the snake, unless one consistently applies the three physical postures, the appearances of primordial wisdom will not manifest. For the moment, as one practices trekchö, the primordial radiance, the spontaneously present precious expanse, is hidden. It is not possible to realize it with the ordinary mind in trekchö, which is like a dark meditation. By making use of the postures and gazes in thögal, the eyes of sublime knowledge (*shes rab kyi mig*) acquire the eye of primordial wisdom (*ye shes kyi spyan*), and consequently the primordial radiance, the spontaneously present precious expanse, can be seen directly with the eye organ.

Second, the key point for the sense door, which allows the visions to manifest, refers to the three gazes. The dharmakāya gaze involves looking with the eyes turned up. Since the dharmakāya has the eye of the dharmatā, looking at the form of the crown protuberance is the key point that purges habitual tendencies downward. The saṃbhogakāya has the eye of primordial wisdom, so looking sideways, right and left, as if checking that the shaft of an arrow is straight, is the key point that serves to mingle samsara and nirvana in the same taste. The nirmāṇakāya has the eye of sublime knowledge, so gazing right down is the key point by which one directly arrives at the visions of primordial wisdom. These constitute the key point for the sense door, the key points of the three gazes, as we find in the *Word-Transcending Root Tantra*:

> The key point for the sense door is to turn one's gaze up, cast it down, or look sideways.

Third is the key point for the speech. The root verse states, "The key point for the speech is to train in breathing gently in and out." First of all, one must keep silent. The root tantra[67] states,

> Rely on training, resting,
> And resolving.

First train in not having any kind of deluded conversation. Then, rest without even reciting mantras or other recitations. Finally, resolve [to remain silent] without even making any signs. The result of doing so is mentioned in *Luminous Expanse*:

> Whoever conquers the key point for the speech
> Exhausts the causes of speech and goes beyond suffering.

In particular, it is important to take long, gentle breaths in and out through the mouth, as Shabkar points out:

> The key point of the breath is to breathe out not through
>   the nose but through the mouth,
> With the teeth and lips slightly parted,
> And to breathe in and out extremely gently.
> This key point of the breath is of great importance.

Fourth is the key point for the mind, for which the root verse says, "The key point for the mind is to settle in a state devoid of thoughts of any kind." This is reflected in *Luminous Expanse*:

> Direct the mind out into space,
> And the inner lamps will manifest.

When one fixes the mind, whose essence is awareness, firmly in the space outside, the empty, luminous, and uncompounded radiance of the lamps inside will shine brightly as the ultimate expanse and awareness unite inseparably. This is the intended meaning of *Highest Wisdom*. And similarly, Shabkar says,

> Third, the key point for the mind is to focus on empty space
> Without changing one's gaze
> And, as if mixing one's mind with space,
> To completely focus one's consciousness.
> As a result, awareness will manifest vividly, clear and empty.

In short, since the body is the door for the performance of karmic deeds, one should maintain the posture without moving, like a human corpse in a charnel ground. Since speech is the door of expression through the breath, one should remain silent, like someone who cannot speak. The mind is the space-like door for thought, and therefore one should let luminosity manifest without trying to contrive one's own mental state. When one makes use of these pith instructions on such extraordinary methods, the impure winds will be sealed by the pure wisdom wind. The luminous visions of the ultimate expanse and disks will increase, and one will gain stability through the key point of slowing down the radiance of awareness in the "prison" [of space]. This is the extraordinary means for doing so.

iii) How the Vision of the Four Lamps Arises as Cause and Result

> The lamp of the empty disks of light,
> The lamp of the utterly pure ultimate expanse,
> The lamp of self-arisen wisdom,
> And that of the far-catching water lasso
> Act as cause and result, associated and connected
>   with one another.
> The cause is the stage of their vision on the path;
> The result is the stage of spontaneous
>   self-manifestation.

What are the four lamps? The lamp of the empty disks of light, the lamp of the utterly pure ultimate expanse, the lamp of self-arisen wisdom, and the lamp of the far-catching water lasso. If, at the present time that one is on the path, one applies the key points of the postures and gazes and practices them, in due course, one will reach the culmination of awareness, and at that time, all appearances will be sealed by the ultimate expanse, and phenomenal appearance will be perceived as nothing but infinite purity. These two—the stage of training at present and the stage of attaining maturity sometime in the future—are associated and connected to each other, manifesting as cause and result in the following way. The cause is the vision of the triad of ultimate expanse, disks, and awareness at the present time on the path. The result is the time when the expanse, disks, and awareness are brought to their maturation and the universe and its inhabitants manifest spontaneously and effortlessly as the buddha fields of the three kāyas, self-arisen and self-manifesting.

iv) How the Four Lamps Make It Possible for the Luminous Appearances to Unfold

> How do the four lamps enable the luminous
>   appearances to unfold?
> The lamp of the empty disks of light
> Is the radiance of the lamp of self-arisen wisdom.
> The lamp of utter purity and the lamp of the water
>   lasso
> Are the conditions for mastering the former two.
> The lamp of the expanse provides the space for
>   empty disks,
> While the lamp of the far-catching water lasso
>   connects and makes them visible.
> The lamp of the empty disks acts as the cause for the
>   lamp of self-arisen wisdom to manifest;
> The lamp of the far-catching water lasso acts as the
>   condition.
> The lamp of the pure expanse acts and appears as the
>   ground for the manifestation.

How the four lamps make it possible for the luminous appearances to unfold is as follows. The lamp of the empty disks of light is the outwardly manifesting radiance of the lamp of self-arisen wisdom. The lamp of the utterly pure ultimate expanse serves as the ground for its manifesting, while the lamp of the far-catching water lasso serves as the door for its manifesting. These two, acting as ground and door and manifesting as such, are the conditions for mastering or bringing to maturity the lamp of the empty disks of light and the lamp of self-arisen wisdom that we have just mentioned. In this way, the lamp of the utterly pure ultimate expanse is what provides the space for the lamp of the empty disks of light, while the lamp of the far-catching water lasso connects and makes distinctly visible the triad of the ultimate expanse, disks, and awareness, meaning that they appear clearly.

The more the lamp of the empty disks of light shines, the more the lamp of self-arisen wisdom (the chains of awareness) matures. Thus, the lamp of the empty disks of light acts as the cause for its manifestation or maturation, and similarly the lamp of the far-catching water lasso acts as the condition, while the lamp of the utterly pure ultimate expanse, like a multicolored brocade being unfolded, acts and appears as the ground for its manifestation.

v) The Main Explanation of the Four Lamps

The main explanation of the four lamps is divided into eight parts: (1) an explanation of the precious heart; (2) the lamp of the smooth, white channel; (3) the lamp of the far-catching water lasso; (4) the lamp of the utterly pure ultimate expanse; (5) the lamp of the empty disks of light; (6) the lamp of self-arisen wisdom; (7) the chains of awareness; and (8) a supplementary explanation of a few points of interest.

(A) An Explanation of the Precious Heart

> In the hollow, blazing jewel of the heart in one's
>   body
> Dwells the primordially pure nature of self-arisen
>   primordial wisdom,
> Empty and unceasingly luminous in character,

Present from the beginning in the guise of a body
   with face and arms.
The means for training in seeing its very appearance
   in reality
Is what is known as the vajra chains of awareness
Or the lamp of self-arisen wisdom.
Its radiance dwells in the middle of the octagonal
   palace of the heart.

Here I will give a little preliminary explanation. Although there
are two explanations—with six lamps and with four—apart from
their being different nominal categories, they are, in fact, the same.
From the point of view of there being six lamps, there are three
lamps that are containers and three that are the contents. The first
three are the lamp of the heart of flesh; the lamp of the smooth,
white channel; and the lamp of the far-catching water lasso. The
three lamps that are the contents are the lamp of the utterly pure
ultimate expanse, the lamp of the empty disks of light, and the
lamp of the vajra chains of awareness.

The first three can be explained by analogy with a tree. The root
corresponds to the lamp of the heart of flesh,[68] the trunk to the
crystal *kati* tube, and the fruit to the lamp of the far-catching water
lasso. At present, while we are on the path, as practitioners meditating, these three count as one, for it is said,

The channel connecting the heart to the eyes
Is the crystal kati tube,
A sphere untainted by blood
Wherein the great primordial wisdom moves.

In the present context, the explanation will be given in terms of
the classification with four lamps. Indeed, many texts, including
the *Word-Transcending Root Tantra*, distinguish four lamps. The
Tantra of Awareness Self-Arisen states,

The four lamps are as follows:
The lamp of the empty disks of light,
The lamp of the expanse of awareness,
The lamp of self-arisen wisdom,
And the lamp of the far-catching water lasso.
These are present in all sentient beings.

Accordingly, here too they will be explained using the classification with four lamps.

In one's body is the hollow, blazing jewel—or the dark-red garnet tent—of one's heart. In its center is a light channel, the crystal kati tube. Within it is the dwelling of mind and awareness, a sphere radiant with five-colored light and termed a "ball of the gathering of the five subtle essences." It is a brilliant five-colored sphere made up of the five essences: the essence of space, deep blue like the color of lapis lazuli; the essence of earth, yellow like the color of amber; the essence of water, white like the color of a conch shell; the essence of fire, red like a ruby; and the essence of wind, green like an emerald. In that expanse of light is what is known as the sphere of the ground of Samantabhadra or the sphere of the indestructible uncontrived state, the primordially pure nature of self-arisen primordial wisdom, or the embodiment of the empty nature and unceasing luminous character. It is present from the very beginning in the guise of a body with face and arms, as we read in the *Word-Transcending Root Tantra*:

In the measureless palace of the heart jewel
Is the aspect of the primordially pure nature,
The radiance of the kāya uniting emptiness and luminosity,
Complete with face and arms, in the guise of the vase body,
Spontaneously present and dwelling in a sphere of light
That clearly appears in the different colors of cognizant
    potency.

And the *All-Illuminating Sphere Tantra* says,

In the measureless palace of the heart jewel
Dwells a tiny body, the size of a sesame seed,
Complete in an expanse of five-colored light.
If one trains, it will appear fully on the path.

It is present simply as the ground for the manifestation of luminosity, without having any inherent existence. As for the means
for training in actually seeing its very appearance, we can call it
"the vajra chains of awareness" or the lamp of self-arisen wisdom—
inner radiance, the lamp of self-arisen wisdom, and the chains of
awareness are differently named aspects of what is in essence the
same thing. Rigdzin Jigme Lingpa writes,

> The vajra chains of awareness, profound insight, appear-
> ing like pearls strung on a thread or floating gold threads
> are what we call the "radiance of wisdom." One should
> understand that these are three aspects distinguished for
> the same thing. If one fails to do so, as the Omniscient
> One says, "What with awareness being referred to some-
> times as 'the lamp of self-arisen wisdom,' sometimes as
> 'the inner radiance,' and at other times as 'chains,' one
> can end up getting quite confused."

The radiance of those same chains, or of that lamp of self-arisen
wisdom, dwells in the middle of the octagonal palace of the heart.[69]

(B) The Lamp of the Smooth, White Channel

> The pure channel known as the crystal kati tube
> Has a very fine root and two wide extremities
> Like the horns of a gaur, ending in the centers of the
>   eyes.

In the center of the dark-red garnet heart are present four wisdom
channels: the great golden kati channel to the east, the crystal kati

tube to the south, the avadhūtī or supremely victorious golden sun to the west, and the channel of naturally open and free emptiness to the north. They are channels of light, extremely pure and clear, free of the defects of blood and lymph, and they remain present in the form of channels for as long as the mind and body stay together. When the mind and body separate, they are pure light.

Of these, the lamp of the smooth, white channel or the pure channel known as the crystal kati tube is very fine at the root and broad at its two extremities, rising from the back of the heart. Four fingers' widths from the apex of the heart, it divides into two. They emerge out of the lattice of channels in the neck and follow the paths of the roma and kyangma. From behind the two ears, the ends of the channels bend like the horns of a gaur[70] and reach the center of the pupils of the eyes where they open out.

There is a point here that is extremely difficult to understand. On the one hand, its root is exceedingly fine, about an eighth of a horse's hair in width. On the other hand, its ends are said to be broad because they apprehend the aspects of samsara and nirvana on the secret path of the precious spontaneously present primordial wisdom. In *Golden Garland* we read,

> The channel that connects the jewel to the ocean
> Is white, smooth, and hollow,
> A sphere untainted by blood,
> Wherein the great primordial wisdom moves.

When the body is first formed, it is formed by the action of water, so that in the knot of the channels in the navel both the eyes of the lamp and the eyes of the elements are first formed, after which the body is produced from the eyes of the elements. And from the eyes of the lamp is produced this channel that reaches the pupils of the eyes, which see the luminous appearances of primordial wisdom. The *Later Tantra of the Heart Essence* states,

The self-arisen channel of the great secret
Connecting the heart to the eyes
Is the crystal kati tube.

According to the most authentic writings, because it is the support of the light channels, it is spoken of as a channel, but in truth it is the pure essence of the wind.

(C) The Lamp of the Far-Catching Water Lasso

In the pupils of the eyes—
A half-white, half-black, watery door—
There is the lamp of the far-catching water lasso.

The lamp of the far-catching water lasso should be understood as referring to the eyes. Perceiving samsara and nirvana, the eyes mediate the vision of both pure and hallucinatory appearances. Since, therefore, all appearances manifest through the pupils of the eyes, which are half white, half black, the eyes are similar to a door. Through the secret path of primordial wisdom, these eyes, which are aqueous in nature (or watery globes), make it possible, or constitute the junction, for the three kāyas to be perceived on the path. They are therefore referred to as the lamp of the far-catching water lasso.

(D) The Lamp of the Utterly Pure Ultimate Expanse

When one looks at the expanse of the sky with half-
    closed eyes,
Though bluish at first, it later appears very purely,
Unfolding as the five-colored radiance of primordial
    wisdom,
And the five lights shine like an unfolded brocade.
The radiance of the kāya of the inner expanse
Manifests like reflections in a mirror.

What does the term "lamp of the utterly pure ultimate expanse" mean? Since the essence of the water element transforms into the radiance of the five lights, it is the "ultimate expanse." Because all the impure deluded appearances related to clinging to substantiality are, from the beginning, utterly pure, it is "utterly pure." And since it displays within the expanse of pure space, it is a "lamp."

Beginning by controlling the key points of the body with the three postures and three gazes, one should look at the sky with one's eyes half-closed. For some people, the five-colored glow may not appear distinctly at first but rather bluish or whitish. For a few people, the five-colored glow appears vividly the first time they look. This is a question of whether or not their channels are in a favorable state. Whichever the case, as one guides the lights with the posture and gaze, in the end the lights manifest very purely: the lamp of the utterly pure ultimate expanse unfolds in the sky, level with the space between one's eyebrows. The radiance of the five lights of primordial wisdom inside manifests outside, and the five lights shine clearly like a brocade being unfolded, manifesting as a bright array of five-colored lights in rainbow patterns, quite stable and unchanging. This is the basis for the appearance, within it, of large and small luminous disks, chains, and so on.

As one becomes increasingly practiced in this lamp of the utterly pure ultimate expanse, there comes a point when the eyes of sublime knowledge will have a clear vision of primordial wisdom so that the colors of the ultimate expanse become more beautiful and clear. The sight of the outer elements appears almost overwhelming to the eye—the essence of space, azure like lapis lazuli; the essence of earth, yellow like amber; the essence of water, white like a conch; the essence of fire, red like ruby; and the essence of wind, green like an emerald. The radiance of the kāya of the inner expanse manifests like reflections in a mirror.

It is necessary to distinguish here between the actual ultimate expanse, the appearance of the expanse, and the disks in the expanse. The actual ultimate expanse refers to the lamp of the utterly pure ultimate expanse, manifesting like lattices and pendants of five-colored light, the designs on a brocade or chessboard. The appearance of the expanse refers to the inconceivable perceptions of the appearances of the ground—the five lights appearing in the form of vertical and horizontal straight bands, curved bands, deities' attributes, and so forth. The disks in the expanse refer to the particular visions, within the actual ultimate expanse, of many different motionless small disks like fish eyes with the colors of the five lights.

(E) The Lamp of the Empty Disks of Light

> **Within the lamp of the utterly pure ultimate**
> **expanse,**
> **The self-experience of awareness,**
> **The lamp of the empty disks,**
> **Like ripples from a thrown stone—**
> **Round disks with rims of five-colored light,**
> **And small ones like fish eyes—fleetingly appears.**

Within the lamp of the utterly pure ultimate expanse, the self-experience of awareness, which is like an unfolded brocade, there appears the lamp of the empty disks, brilliant, perfectly round lights,[71] looking like the ripples made when a stone is thrown into water. As it is said,

> Within that, the lamp of the empty disks appears
> Like the designs made by a stone thrown into a pond,
> Indistinct at first
> But eventually clear disks of light.

Accordingly, within the ultimate expanse and the appearance of that expanse, there appears the lamp of the empty disks, the essence of the five subtle inner elements. At first, they appear indistinctly, but gradually, with practice, they manifest as round disks with rims of five-colored light, like the eye in a peacock's feather. Of the inner elements, the essence of the mind is dark blue like liquid lapis lazuli. The essence of flesh is yellow like liquid saffron. The essence of blood is white like cow's milk. The essence of warmth is red like vermilion. And the essence of the breath is green like the water in the ocean or the grass in a meadow. All of these appear, shining brightly.

There are three categories of lamp of the empty disks: the still disk, or rather sphere, of the ground; the gross, causal disk, or rather essence-drop; and the disk, or rather sphere, of the self-arisen result.[72] The first of these is the sphere of the indestructible uncontrived nature in the center of the heart. It is also called "the sphere of the ground of Samantabhadra." The second refers to the two essential constituents, white and red, present in the roma and kyangma channels, and they are called "the gross, causal essence-drops." The third refers to the extremely clear and brilliant round disks of five-colored light that are the pure primordial radiance of ultimate reality and that are directly perceptible to the sense organ. They are called "the spheres of the self-arisen result" because they are the creative power or result of self-arisen awareness manifesting outwardly.

In brief, the disks appear momentarily, very fine and of no fixed size—large, circular disks with rims of five-colored light, which, as they grow larger, are the size of a shield or an arm span in circumference, and small disks like the eye of a needle or a fish eye, and so on.

In general, all the manifesting aspects of the ultimate expanse, disks, and awareness dwell inside the light channel, the crystal kati tube, in the light expanse of five essences, the sphere of the ground of Samantabhadra (or sphere of the indestructible uncontrived nature). When one masters them with the gazes and looks with the eye of sublime knowledge, they become manifest within the channel inside. They have no existence as objects outside. To consider that the appearances of the ultimate expanse are outside and that awareness is inside, and to think that all the luminous appearances exist somewhere else, will lead to the enormous error of dualistic apprehension, where the empty luminosity of awareness and the manifest luminosity of appearing spontaneous presence are separated.

(F) The Lamp of Self-Arisen Wisdom

> Inner awareness, extremely limpid, clear, and
> unceasing,
> Manifesting free of limits and beyond extremes—
> That is the lamp of self-arisen wisdom.

Inner awareness, extremely limpid and clear, or the inner ultimate expanse, utterly pure, empty, luminous, and unceasing, and manifesting free of limits and beyond extremes—that self-arisen awareness is the lamp of self-arisen wisdom. It is the ground for the manifestation of all the lamps. Without it, it is impossible for there to be the other five lamps, and since it is the great wisdom that knows all the lamps, it is called the lamp of self-arisen wisdom.

In terms of function, there are said to be four categories of this wisdom: liberating wisdom, moving wisdom, gathering wisdom, and discriminating wisdom. The wisdom that dissolves ignorance into the expanse of awareness is liberating wisdom. The wisdom that moves the five kāyas in the expanse of primordial purity and awareness in the expanse of primordial wisdom is moving wisdom. The wisdom that gathers the five elements into the expanse of the five essences, gathers the five aggregates into the expanse of the five kāyas, and gathers the five kāyas into the expanse of awareness is gathering wisdom. And the wisdom that distinguishes awareness and ignorance, realization and lack of realization, defilements and primordial wisdom, samsara and nirvana, and so forth is discriminating wisdom.

Generally speaking, the lamp of self-arisen wisdom has three aspects: nature, creative power, and radiance. Of these, its nature is the knowing aspect of empty, luminous, and unceasing inner awareness, which, when one adopts the key points of the three gazes and concentrates on the lamp of the empty disks of light, emerges clear and naked. It is the primordial wisdom that knows the nature of phenomena as they are. Through its creative power, the wisdom of outer luminosity bursts forth from the treasury of the expanse of awareness. This is the wisdom that sees all phenomena in their multiplicity, clearly and distinctly. The radiance is a case of the result being named after the cause: it refers to the vajra chains of the radiance of awareness. In this regard, as has been clearly explained above, the three terms, inner radiance, the lamp of self-arisen wisdom, and the chains of awareness, should be understood as being differently named aspects for what is essentially the same thing.

In short, through the profound means that is the key point of the gaze, when one concentrates on the lamp of the utterly pure ultimate expanse using the lamp of the far-catching water lasso, one creates the causal factor for the qualities of precious spontaneous presence, and by applying the key points of the sense door, visual field or object, wind, and awareness, one creates the secondary cause for the eye of wisdom. Through this connection, the appearances of the ultimate expanse and the lamp of the empty disks of light, together with the chains, manifest.

Dudjom Lingpa makes the following analogy. The light channel, the crystal kati tube, is like a vessel. The lamp of the utterly pure ultimate expanse is like its contents. The lamp of the empty disks of light is like their essence. And the lamp of self-arisen wisdom, the ground for the manifestation of all, is like their quintessence.

As for the qualities that come from seeing these, seeing the lamp of the utterly pure ultimate expanse is equivalent to seeing the ultimate Akaniṣṭha,[73] which is the self-experience of awareness. Seeing the lamp of the empty disks of light is equivalent to seeing the spontaneously present measureless palace of great bliss. And seeing the vajra chains that are the radiance of awareness is equivalent to seeing the sixth buddha, the great Vajradhara, in person.

(G) The Chains of Awareness

> Within it, there appear the vajra chains of profound
>   insight,
> Like golden threads and necklaces of pearls and flowers.
> They are the radiance of the lamp of inner awareness
>   shining outside.
> Holding them captive in the enclosure of the
>   ultimate expanse and disks,
> One blends the expanse, disks, and awareness into one.
> In the beginning, they shake and tremble,
> One cannot keep them still for an instant,
> And awareness, agitated by the winds, loses control.

Thus, from within the lamp of self-arisen wisdom the "vajra chains" of profound insight manifest like spun-gold threads, stretched strings of crystal, knotted horse hairs, pearls threaded on silk, stretched chains, flowers strung into garlands. These are the radiance of the awareness of the inner expanse, the lamp of the utterly pure ultimate expanse, shining outwardly.

At first, before one has become used to the practice, they appear to shake and shimmer like a mirage. It is said,

> What we call the vajra chains of awareness
> Are like knotted horse hairs, threads of gold,
> Pearl necklaces, flower garlands,
> And chains. At first they appear like mirages,
> Trembling and indistinct.
> The key point is to guide them with one's gaze,
> Enclosing them within the fence of the ultimate expanse,
> And to look without moving.

As a sign that one must gain freedom in dependence on the key point of the winds, the chains appear to come and go. As a sign that one must gain freedom in dependence on the key point of the channels, the chains are fine and crooked. And as a sign that one must gain freedom in dependence on the key point of the essence-drops, they appear ornamented by disks of light like fish eyes on the bends of the crooked lines.

The lamp of the utterly pure ultimate expanse, which is like an unfolded brocade, and the lamp of the empty disks—that is, the various large and small disks of light within it—constitute a sort of enclosure. Using one's gaze to guide the vajra chains that are the radiance of awareness into this enclosure, one focuses intensely on them, holding them unmoving. One holds them captive, so to speak. As is stated in *Luminous Expanse,*

> The key point of awareness on which one must rely
> Is to take the chains captive, to make them firm by slowing
>   them down.

Accordingly, when one practices with the ultimate expanse, disks, and awareness blended into one, if one gets lost in examining and distinguishing the luminous appearances, one will slip into thinking of the chains as existing substantially. This will be a hindrance and an error, so it is very important to not have any clinging, for all the luminous appearances are one's own nature manifesting clearly by itself.

In the beginning, before one becomes used to this, the chains shake and tremble like a mirage; one cannot keep them still for a second, and one's awareness, agitated by the winds, loses control. They appear successively like swiftly flying birds, wandering deer, and bees hovering over a patch of flowers. At such times it is important to slow them down and not let them go outside the enclosure of the ultimate expanse, as is stated in the *Array of Studded Jewels Tantra*:

> If you wish to look at the heart of all the buddhas, look at
>   the body of the vajra chains.
> If you wish to realize the wisdom mind of all the buddhas,
>   do not separate from the vajra chains.

And,

> If you wish to master the whole of the secret primordial
> wisdom, look at the rays of vajra chains.

Through one's relying on the pith instructions on these extraordinary means, the impure winds are sealed with the pure wind of
primordial wisdom. This is the key point for increasing the luminous visions of the ultimate expanse and disks and slowing down
the radiance of awareness in the enclosure of the expanse. It is thus
the extraordinary means for attaining stability.

In short, the ground of the training being the sugata essence, the
object of training being the six lamps, and the agent of the training
being the key points of the sense door, visual field or object, wind,
and awareness, the result of the training is that one completes the
four visions and attains buddhahood in the inner luminosity of the
youthful vase body.

    In general, as a basis for thögal, it is necessary to achieve con-
fidence in the view of trekchö, and therefore, whatever manifestations arise, if one loses the grounding of trekchö—that is,
awareness—things will go very wrong, as is mentioned in *The
Treasury of Words and Meanings*:

> The visions of thögal must first manifest. During the
> meditation, there must be no clinging. Afterward these
> visions must be exhausted, because awareness joined
> with wind must keep to its natural state. The aspect of
> wind has to be purified. After the aspect of the radi-
> ance of awareness has been increased, it must then be
> exhausted in the inner expanse. It is difficult to realize
> the true sense of this. It took me a long time, and that
> realization was thanks to the kindness of my teacher.

(H) A Supplementary Explanation of a Few Points of Interest

> The contributory factors for the visions
> Are the sun, moon, lamps, crystals, and so forth:
> These props are used by day and night
> To lead and refine [the rays] from them.
> The visions arise from the far-catching lasso alone
> Or from all the sense organs.
> Focusing on the appearance of the four lamps,
> One should concentrate on maturing awareness.
> The four lamps are not to be taken separately:
> They are like the body and its limbs, like the three
>   kāyas.
> By failing to understand the point of the lamp of
>   self-arisen wisdom,
> Great meditators fixate [on the lamps as different]
> And mostly tire themselves out.
> Even if they meditate in darkness for a hundred
>   years,
> How could that free them from the perilous path of
>   duality?

As contributory factors for the appearance of all the manifestation aspects of thögal, such as the triad of the ultimate expanse, disks, and awareness, one needs, during the day, to look at the sun's rays and, at night, to look at the moon. Shabkar says,[74]

> If looking at the sun during the day
> Makes the eyes heat up,
> Looking at the moon at night
> Is the remedy for dispelling heat in the eyes.

Similarly, one should be diligent in the means for intensifying the visions by looking at *aloke* offering lamps or lights,[75] rainbow crystals, and so forth. In particular, unless beginners make use of these contributory objects all the time, day and night, the visions cannot manifest, so it is important to rely on props that help give rise to the visions, like the sun, moon, and rainbow crystals, and to lead and refine the rays from them.

Where the root verse says, "from the far-catching lasso alone or . . . ," it means that beginners need to look, using only the far-catching lasso—that is, the eye. But apart from that, it is wrong to imagine that one always has to see through the sense door of the eyes alone. For, as we read in *Highest Wisdom*,

> Nevertheless, the key point of the sense door is not limited only to this. When one sees the ultimate expanse, which is the goal of the practice, then, as it is said in the *Necklace of Pearls Tantra*,
>
>> The chains of awareness devoid of dualistic cognition
>> Appear through the pure door of great bliss.
>
> And the same text states that from the central light channel, the empty radiance of the nature manifests, and from inside the lung channel the radiance of awareness related to cognizant power arises, and so on. Therefore, as it is said in *Sun, Moon, Planets, and Stars*, those whose understanding is limited to identifying the two channels of the ordinary eyes as the path of the luminous visions do not understand this.

When one reaches the culmination of awareness in thögal, [the visions] manifest from all the sense organs, as it is said:

> When one reaches the climax of awareness in thögal,
> Through each of the pores on one's body
> One sees infinite buddha fields;
> One sees boundless realms of six classes of beings too.

If they can manifest like that even through each of one's pores, suffice it to say that they manifest through all one's sense organs.

By focusing on and practicing the key points of sense door, visual field or object, wind, and awareness as the means for making the four lamps manifest, in due course, when awareness comes to maturity, the five aggregates are not abandoned but appear as the buddhas of the five families, and the five elements are not abandoned but appear as the five female buddhas. Phenomenal existence manifests as infinite purity. One should concentrate, therefore, on the means for attaining that.

Apart from the fact that the four lamps are but the external arising of the creative power of the inner expanse, the lamp of self-arisen awareness, they are not to be considered as separate. The four lamps are of the same nature as the lamp of self-arisen wisdom, but they are distinguished separately in being different aspects of it. To make an analogy, the lamp of self-arisen wisdom is explained as being like the body and the other lamps as its limbs. But body and limbs are both part of the same mass and no different from it. Another analogy that illustrates this is that of there being a single awareness, whose empty nature is the dharmakāya, its luminous character the saṃbhogakāya, and its multifarious manifestations the nirmāṇakāya. But in truth these three kāyas are not distinct from the sole awareness. As it is said,

> The three kāyas are shown through different introductions,
> But in fact they are the same ultimate expanse. Do not be deluded
> By considering them otherwise, as distinct, O child of my heart!

So whether they are explained as four lamps or six, they are nothing other than the manifestation of the creative power of the lamp of self-arisen wisdom, self-cognizing awareness. Nevertheless, it seems that there are great meditators who, because they are confused and do not understand this point, think of the four lamps as distinct, external entities and, as a result of their fixation, mostly tire themselves out. As Dudjom Lingpa says,

> One should consider everything as awareness inside. If one considers that all the manifestations exist elsewhere, one will separate the luminosity of empty awareness and the luminosity of appearing spontaneous presence, and the terrible obscuring error of dualistic clinging will occur.

With such an error, even if one does dark meditation for a hundred years, how could one's mindstream ever be freed from the perilous path of duality? It is impossible.

b) How One Progresses through the Four Visions of Thögal

This section is divided into (1) a brief introduction and (2) a detailed explanation.

i) Brief Introduction

> With the lamp of the far-catching water lasso,
> One has the vision of dharmatā in reality.
> With the lamp of the empty disks,
> One has the vision of the enhanced experiences of
> awareness.
> With the lamp of the utterly pure ultimate expanse,
> One has the vision of the climax of awareness.
> With the lamp of self-arisen wisdom,
> One is brought to the level of the exhaustion of
> phenomena in the dharmatā.

As a result of one's meditating using the key points of the sense door, visual field or object, wind, and awareness together with the three postures and the three gazes, a time will come when, through the path of the lamp of the far-catching water lasso, one will have the vision of the dharmatā in reality, with as many as three luminous disks joined together. Then, as one meditates in stages, relying on the contributory conditions for the lamp of the empty disks of light, there will appear within the disks the tiny forms of deities. When this happens, one has reached the level of the vision of the enhanced experiences of awareness. After that, if one goes on practicing, all one's perceptions are sealed by the lamp of the utterly pure ultimate expanse, and at that time, all appearances manifest as deities and buddha fields. This is the vision of the climax of awareness. And when one practices even more, one makes manifest the path of the lamp of self-arisen wisdom so that one is brought to the level where all appearances of phenomena are exhausted in the expanse of the primordially pure ultimate reality. This is known as the vision of the exhaustion of phenomena in the dharmatā.

ii) Detailed Explanation

The detailed explanation consists of four parts: (1) the vision of the dharmatā in reality, (2) the vision of the enhanced experiences of awareness, (3) the vision of the climax of awareness, and (4) the vision of the exhaustion of phenomena in the dharmatā.

(A) The Vision of the Dharmatā in Reality

> One realizes the four visions
> By implementing the key points.
> The chains of awareness,
> Like scattered knots in horsehair
> And clusters of flowers,
> Appear indistinctly, shifting and quivering:
> Sometimes ones sees them, sometimes not.
> This is said to be the stage of seeing the dharmatā in
>   reality.

The way one realizes these four visions by implementing the key points of the thögal practice of spontaneous presence is as described in the *Word-Transcending Root Tantra*:

> From this, there will occur four visions.
> With the vision of the dharmatā in reality,
> One is beyond words that grasp at mental fabrications.
> With the vision of the enhanced experiences of awareness,
> Deluded appearances subside,
> And one realizes the primordial wisdom of the bardo.
> With the vision of the climax of awareness,
> One achieves the realization in which the appearances of
>   the three kāyas on the path are transcended.
> With the vision of the exhaustion of phenomena in the
>   dharmatā,
> One severs the continuity of the three worlds of samsara.

As it is said, in thögal, the sphere in one's heart that is made up of the five essences and is the support for the sugatagarbha manifests as outwardly radiating luminosity. First, there appears spontaneously and vividly the lamp of the utterly pure ultimate expanse, like an unfurled multicolored brocade curtain, still and bright. Within it there appears the lamp of the empty disks of light—three connected disks the size of fish eyes in five colors. And within the expanse and disks, there appears the radiance of awareness—inexpressible, primordially pure awareness, empty and luminous—manifesting as the vajra chains of the awareness of profound insight, appearing indistinctly like knotted horse hairs, plaited golden threads, pearls strung on silk, and clusters of flowers. At first, when one looks, they shift and quiver, so that sometimes one sees them, sometimes one does not. In *Vajra Verses on the Fundamental Nature* we read,

> The radiance of awareness, vajra chains,
> Appears as pearls strung on silk

Or as pure, refined brilliance.
This is the path of the great primordial wisdom
Of the buddhas, past, present, and future.
Therefore, for whoever sees them and hits the key point,
The three worlds are no more.

One can make the analogy of a face and its reflection in a mirror. The actual radiance of the ground awareness is like the face, and the vajra chains of awareness are like its reflections in a mirror. Here it is important to understand that inasmuch as they are connected, one arising from the other, the result is being named after the cause. In short, when the vajra chains that are the radiance of awareness enter the enclosure of the lamp of the utterly pure ultimate expanse, and three connected luminous disks (symbolizing the three kāyas) manifest continuously, this is said to be the stage of seeing the dharmatā in reality. It has been taught that at this stage, when one dies, one will never fall back in the three worlds of samsara and will be liberated in a nirmāṇakāya buddha field of luminous character.[76] This is the point at which one has attained the first bodhisattva level according to the sūtra vehicle and the level of vidyādhara with a karmic body according to the secret mantras.

(B) The Vision of the Enhanced Experiences of Awareness

Circular disks of five-colored light,
Straight bands, vertical and horizontal, and so on,
Separate from between the eyes,
And within the expanse of the sky and disks
Appear half bodies of deities and the like.
Deluded perceptions diminish.
This is said to be the stage of the enhanced
    experiences of awareness.

People who aspire to this swift path of the secret mantras, the Vajrayāna, completely abandon samsaric activities and practice without laziness or procrastination. If, with faith and devotion to their teacher, they invoke the latter's wisdom mind, all their experiences will develop more and more, like the waxing moon, and thus this stage is named "the enhanced experiences of awareness," as is stated in *Luminous Expanse*:

> As the visions increase,
> It is important to distinguish the enhancement of
>   experiences.

There is a distinction in the enhancement of experiences between the experiences of the ordinary mind (*shes nyams*) and the experiences of awareness (*snang nyams*). With regard to the experiences of the ordinary mind, the gathering of mind and wind gives rise to numerous experiences, pleasant and unpleasant; and all sorts of unpredictable experiences of the ordinary mind manifest, such as bliss, clarity, and absence of thought, and smoke, mirages, and others of the ten signs of purification [of the wind in the central channel], and so on. All these are the products of the deceptive mind, and they should not be used as a measure of progress on the path. What, then, should one use to measure one's progress? In the Luminous Great Perfection, it is the experiences of awareness that one needs to take into account. A tantra states,

> When the experience of emptiness manifests inside,
> Primordial wisdom appears outside.

When one's mind realizes the nature of dharmatā within, its radiance, the primordial wisdom of the luminous character, appears outside: circular disks of five-colored light and, as the display of the ultimate expanse, straight bands of light, both vertical and horizontal, and all kinds of images like stūpas, thousand-petaled lotuses, and palaces, the tips of spears, wheels, curved knives, crossed vajras, letters and syllables, lattices and pendants, checkered patterns, and so forth. All these appear in unpredictable fashion. As they grow more and more, they constitute what is called "the enhanced experiences of awareness." In the *Word-Transcending Root Tantra* we read,

> The vision of the enhanced experiences of awareness
> Consists of the colors of primordial wisdom projected
>   outside
> In the form of vertical and horizontal straight lines,
> Multifarious disks of light and forms of deities.

And *Highest Wisdom* speaks of manifestations such as straight bands of five-colored light, horizontal and vertical, groups of circles, stūpas, thousand-petaled lotuses, palaces, [rays] like the tips of spears, checkered patterns, and so forth.

As for the vajra chains at that time, it is said,

> At the stage of enhanced experiences, they become slightly
>   more stable;
> They are like tiny pearls strung on silk.
> As they mature, they gradually increase and become more
>   stable.

According to Rigdzin Jigme Lingpa, at this time, if the manifestations are predominantly white, one looks to the right; if they are mainly yellow, one looks up; if mainly green, one looks to the left; if mostly red, one looks down; if mostly blue, one looks in the middle; and if five-colored, one looks at where they are.

Similarly, it is said in *Highest Wisdom* that when the manifestations of the ultimate expanse appear as horizontal lines, one looks in front; when vertical, one looks down; if they manifest as squares, one looks to the right; if semicircular, one looks up; if triangular, one looks down; if circular, one looks to the left; and if they manifest as palaces, one looks in no specific direction.

It is said that if the best, most diligent practitioners practice like this, it takes five days to progress from the visions of the stage below to those of the stage above. For middling practitioners it takes seven days, and for the least diligent ones twenty-one days.

When one looks at the display of the ultimate expanse on the level in between one's eyebrows, at first the manifestations are like a white letter *naro*[77] and like the shape of a bird flying in the distance. As one trains in this, the display of the ultimate expanse separates from the forehead and appears as utterly vast as the sky. Within the expanse of the sky and the disks of light, one sees tiny forms of deities, the head of Vajrasattva and half the face, and then half the body, and eventually the whole body. It is at this point that one has completed the vision of the enhanced experiences of awareness. At that time, deluded perceptions diminish and one's inner channels dissolve into light. On the secret level, defilements subside in their own nature, and the whole seat and deity's body manifest. At this stage, when one dies, one is liberated without going through the bardo. This stage is said to be the point at which one attains the fifth bodhisattva level, Difficult to Train, on the sūtra path and the level of vidyādhara with power over life on the mantra path.

All this is said to be the stage of the enhanced experiences of awareness. When someone on this stage dies, they immediately attain buddhahood.

(C) The Vision of the Climax of Awareness

> In the center of circular disks of five-colored light
>   filling space,
> The principal peaceful and wrathful deities and
>   their entourage all appear.
> Samsara and nirvana are realized as the great
>   infinite purity.
> All attainments grow to completion like the full moon.
> This is said to be the stage of the climax of awareness.

In the fundamental nature of the ground, awareness, the three kāyas are primordially present and complete. Therefore, all the qualities of the saṃbhogakāya, without exception or omission, like the reflection of a face in a mirror, are now truly perfect and complete in this experience on the path. This is the meaning of reaching the climax of awareness.

Here, when all phenomena are sealed by the ultimate expanse, the appearances of earth, water, fire, and wind will be purified in their own nature. In the *Tantra of the Blazing Relics* it is said,

> For those who train in light,
> The appearances in their field of vision
> Of the four elements, earth, water, fire, and wind, will fade
> And they will gradually experience the five colors.

The five aggregates, without being rejected, are perceived as the five families of buddhas, and the five elements, without being rejected, are perceived as the five female buddhas. The manifestations of luminosity arise everywhere, and space is filled with circular five-colored disks, in the middle of which there appear all the principal peaceful and wrathful deities and their entourages, without exception or omission. One's own body too is perceived as the deities of the three seats complete, and everything in phenomenal existence, samsara and nirvana, is realized as the great infinite purity.

At that time, all attainments grow to completion, like the full moon. This is said to be the stage of the climax of awareness. One has the capacity to have dominion over any appearance whatsoever, one receives the empowerment of great light rays, and—with every part of one's body emanating the nirmāṇakāyas of luminous character, the nirmāṇakāya guides of beings, and the diversified nirmāṇakāyas[78]—one is able to benefit beings on an infinite scale. Besides this, one is endowed with inconceivable qualities—the vision of countless buddha fields, the wisdom that knows all phenomena simultaneously, mastery of infinite doors of concentration, and so on. And at this time, when one dies, one attains buddhahood in the saṃbhogakāya. This is equivalent to attain-

ing the eighth bodhisattva level on the sūtra path and the level of
mahāmudrā vidyādhara on the mantra path.

(D) The Vision of the Exhaustion of Phenomena in the Dharmatā

> All appearances are gathered into the great sphere.
> Like the moon dissolving into space at new moon,
> The appearances of phenomena dissolve into the
>   expanse of dharmatā.
> Their exhaustion is not nothingness
> But the transfer of appearances toward emptiness.
> One has seized the inner luminosity,
> The everlasting domain of the youthful vase body.
> This is said to be the stage of the great exhaustion of
>   phenomena beyond mind.

With regard to this, the *Word-Transcending Root Tantra* states,

> With the vision of the exhaustion of phenomena in the
>   dharmatā,
> The experiences [of the vision of the climax of awareness]
>   disappear into emptiness:
> The body comes to exhaustion, the sense objects come to
>   exhaustion,
> And freed of all deluded thoughts,
> One is left speechless.

All appearances are gathered into the great sphere of primordial
purity, dharmatā. Like the moon, which is full on the fifteenth day
of the lunar month and then dissolves into the great emptiness of
space at the time of the new moon and becomes invisible, all the
visions of deities and buddha fields at the climax of awareness gradually dissolve. Beginning with the buddha fields dissolving into the
measureless palaces, the palaces dissolve into the deities, the deities

into the disks of light, and the disks of light dissolve into the inner expanse. In the same way that, in the texts of Mahāyoga, the whole visualization in the generation stage finally dissolves into the emptiness of the perfection stage, all the appearances of phenomena dissolve into the expanse of dharmatā.

The power of the pure dharmatā is such that, on the outer level, all hallucinatory appearances of the sense objects cease. On the inner level, the deluded, conceptual mind, along with the habitual tendencies of mental factors, cease by themselves. On the secret level, all the visions of luminosity dissolve and are exhausted in the utterly inexpressible expanse of the dharmatā. Although we use the term "exhaustion" here, the exhaustion of phenomena in the dharmatā is not an absolute nothingness, as when a fire is extinguished or water dries up, or like the horn of a rabbit. Rather, appearances have been transferred toward emptiness. Let us make an analogy: although the full moon and new moon appear to wax and wane, in fact there is no increase or diminution happening. And although the light of a crystal is absorbed within, when the sun shines on it, it becomes brilliantly iridescent. Similarly, although the radiance of awareness subsides into the ultimate expanse, it is present as the indivisible nature of primordial purity and spontaneous presence, and the everlasting domain in the expanse of the youthful vase body, the inner luminosity absorbed within yet not obscured, is seized. Sense objects appearing outside, one's material body inside, and the movements of the karmic wind in between are brought to maturity as the play of luminosity, and one realizes the rainbow body of the great transformation. Thus it is said that one has arrived at the stage of the great exhaustion of phenomena beyond mind.

At that moment, one acquires the four great states of confidence, free of fear. One is completely absorbed in the all-pervading state free of limits and beyond extremes that is the vast space of the vajra queen, the primordial wisdom of the nature pure from the beginning and free from the eight conceptual extremes, the empty expanse endowed with the three doors of perfect liberation. In a tantra we find,

> With the vision of the exhaustion of phenomena in the
>   dharmatā
> One will attain the result, the state of no-action of the
>   Great Perfection.
> When one reaches this final goal,
> There is no other nirvana to be sought.

Here, the exhaustion of phenomena in the dharmatā on this path of the Great Perfection is equivalent to attaining the tenth bodhisattva level, Cloud of Dharma, on the sūtra path and attaining the supreme level of spontaneously accomplished vidyādhara on the mantra path.

c) Four Supporting Pith Instructions

There are four sets of supporting pith instructions, as mentioned in *Luminous Expanse*:

> For this, there are four supporting pith instructions.
> Without their backing, nothing is possible.

As it says, these instructions are indispensable, for if someone who is truly practicing the profound thögal practice of spontaneous presence in the Luminous Great Perfection does not have them, there is no way they can succeed. These instructions concern (1) laying the foundation [for the stability of ultimate expanse-awareness] with three kinds of motionlessness, (2) grasping the extent [of this stability] with the three kinds of settling, (3) nailing it with the three kinds of attainment, and (4) showing the perfect freedom through four kinds of confident certainty.

i) Laying the Foundation with the Three Kinds of Motionlessness

Then there are the supporting instructions called
"Laying the foundation with the three kinds of
motionlessness":
The body is kept motionless
So that awareness rests without wavering.
The eyes are kept motionless
So that the ultimate expanse and awareness do not separate.
The winds and awareness are kept motionless
So that luminosity stabilizes and increases.

The first of the four supporting instructions, "laying the foundation with the three kinds of motionlessness," is very important, as is mentioned in the *Word-Transcending Root Tantra*:

By laying the foundation with the three kinds of
motionlessness,
One will achieve the key point of wind and awareness.

It is necessary to maintain the three physical postures without moving so that one strikes at the key point of the channels and winds, and awareness rests without wavering from the ultimate expanse. One should keep one's two eyes motionless in the three gazes so that the ultimate expanse and awareness do not separate. And one should keep the breath relaxed and the vajra chains, the radiance of awareness, motionless so that luminosity becomes perfectly stable and greatly increases. Jigme Lingpa writes,

When the body does not move from its posture, the winds
in the channels naturally slow down.
When the eyes do not move from their gaze, the visions are
enhanced.
And when the mind does not move from the uncontrived
state, the ultimate expanse and awareness are united.

ii) Grasping the Extent [of Stability] with the Three Kinds of Settling

This is divided into (1) the main explanation and (2) incidental points

(A) The Main Explanation

> The extent [of stability] is grasped with the three
> kinds of settling:
> As appearances settle, the ultimate expanse and
> awareness will be free of coming and going.
> As the aggregates settle, deluded perceptions will be
> purified in the ultimate expanse.
> As the wind-mind settles, thoughts will come to
> exhaustion.

The way in which the extent [of stability of ultimate expanse-awareness] is grasped with the three kinds of settling—outer, inner, and secret—is as follows. When the wind that gives rise to the movements of outer appearances comes to exhaustion and settles, the ultimate expanse and awareness are free from coming and going and settle for long periods of time. When the wind that gives rise to the movement of the inner aggregates comes to exhaustion and one's body settles without moving, one ceases to engage in samsaric activities, and deluded perceptions are purified in the ultimate expanse. And, on the secret level, when the wind-mind that gives rise to the movement of thoughts subsides and settles in the ultimate expanse, thoughts come to exhaustion and their movements are no longer possible. The increase of the ultimate expanse and disks of light is complete and the buddha fields reach their full perfection.

(B) Incidental Points

Incidental to grasping the extent of the stability of ultimate expanse-awareness with the three kinds of settling are the following points, which can be grouped into grasping the extent in relation to dreams and observing the signs related to the activities of the three doors. These are to be found in the *Word-Transcending Root Tantra* of the Heart Essence:

> From grasping the extent with the three kinds of settling,
> Dreams will stop and one will recognize
> Signs and degrees related to the body, speech, and
>   mind.

(1) Dreams

For the first of these, the root text says,

> **As for grasping the extent of stability in terms of
>   one's dreams:**
> **For those of highest faculties,**
> **Dreams are purified in the ultimate expanse and
>   luminosity manifests.**
> **Those of middling faculties recognize their nature**
> **And assume and transform different forms in their
>   dreams.**
> **For those of least ability, bad dreams cease.**

When the three kinds of settling are mastered, dreams are used to grasp the extent of stability in ultimate expanse-awareness. As a sign that those with sharp faculties and the greatest diligence have cut their connection with karmic actions and habitual tendencies and will be freed in this life, their dreams are purified in the ultimate expanse. Even their sleep manifests as the great bliss of luminosity. Those of middling faculties recognize whatever they dream as dream. Free of fixation to their true existence—and gaining mastery in assuming, transforming, and multiplying forms in their dream—they recognize their own nature of awareness. Those of least faculties have cut the stream of bad dreams, karma, and habitual tendencies and will only have good dreams. Thus, the *Tantra of the Secret Word* states,

> For the best, there is manifestation; for the middling,
>   recognition;
> And for the least, virtuous dreams.

And Jigme Lingpa says,

> As a sign that those with sharp faculties and the greatest diligence have cut their connection with karmic deeds and habitual tendencies and will attain buddhahood in this life, their dreams are purified into the ultimate expanse and they recognize luminosity.
>
> Those of middling faculties recognize their dreams as dream, and as a result of their certain proficiency in the manifestation and transformation of forms in their dreams, they will attain buddhahood in the bardo.
>
> Those of most modest faculties will cease to have bad dreams and have only good dreams. They will find relief in nirmāṇakāya buddha fields of luminous character.

(2) Signs

Second, with regard to the signs that one observes related to the activities of one's three doors, there is (1) a brief introduction and (2) a detailed explanation.

(a) Brief Introduction

> The signs of proficiency in the four visions
> Manifest on the level of body, speech, and mind.

When one practices the ground and path together—the trekchö view of primordial purity and the thögal path of luminosity—signs of proficiency in the four visions manifest progressively. These signs—physical, verbal, and mental—are as follows.

(b) Detailed Explanation

There are (1) three signs associated with the vision of the dharmatā in reality, (2) three signs associated with the enhanced experiences of awareness, (3) three signs associated with the climax of awareness, and (4) three signs associated with the exhaustion of phenomena in the dharmatā.

(i) The Three Signs Associated with the Dharmatā in Reality

> Three signs are associated with the vision of
> dharmatā in reality:
> Physically, one is like a tortoise placed in a metal
> bowl;
> Verbally, one is as if mute, with nothing to say;
> And mentally, one stays put, like a bird caught in a
> trap.

The three signs related to the vision of dharmatā in reality are as follows. As a result of one's body having been matured by the vase empowerment, one's limbs are infused with the absence of all activity, so that one's body is like a tortoise placed in a smooth metal bowl—it stays where it is, without doing anything or moving around. Since one's speech is infused with the radiance of the pure basis of expression of the Great Perfection, one has no wish to speak, like a mute person who has nothing to say. And similarly, since one's mind is infused with the Great Perfection path of natural openness and freedom free of clinging—that is, the self-subsiding of thoughts—it is like a bird[79] caught in a trap, and one's consciousness remains firm and steady wherever it is focused.

(ii) The Three Signs Associated with the Enhanced Experiences of Awareness

> Three signs are associated with the enhanced
>   experiences of awareness:
> Physically, one loses one's self-respect, like someone
>   racked by illness;
> Verbally, one speaks gibberish, like a madman;
> And mentally, one is like someone who has been
>   poisoned.

As a result of the wind-mind dissolving into the central channel, one's body is infused with the great equality for which there is neither good nor bad so that, physically, one is like someone who loses their self-respect, and one has no inclination to make oneself look nice, as if one were racked by illness. Because one's speech has been purified by the secret empowerment, it is infused with the Great Perfection's transcendence of all affirmation and negation so that one speaks gibberish, with no relevance to anything, like the verbal outpourings of a madman. Since all the thoughts related to mental factors have been naturally purified in the ultimate expanse that knows no delusion, it is no longer possible for one's mind to be deluded in samsara, like someone who has been crazed by poison seven times and who cannot be poisoned further.

(iii) The Three Signs Associated with the Climax of Awareness

> Three signs are associated with the climax of
>   awareness:
> Physically, one moves forward like an elephant
>   mired in a swamp;
> One's speech is as beautiful as that of a young
>   kumbhāṇḍa;
> And mentally, one is like someone who has
>   recovered from smallpox.

The power of the wisdom empowerment affects the channels and winds and increases the strength of the wisdom channels and winds so that, physically, one can pass freely and unhindered through the five elements, like an elephant, which, even when mired in a swamp, has the strength to extract itself on its own. Similarly, as the expressive functions of one's speech are infused with the Great Perfection, beyond description by word, and as they are connected with the union of wisdom and compassion, whatever the yogi says inspires faith and pure perception in others and benefits all beings—just as, when the children of the kumbhāṇḍas sing with their beautiful voices, other beings cannot but be utterly enchanted. Since one's mind is infused with, and has awoken to, the fact that one's nature is primordially pure and free from the beginning and so does not need to be freed again, it is impossible for it to revert to samsara, like someone who has recovered from smallpox and is immune to contracting it again.

(iv) The Three Signs Associated with the Exhaustion of Phenomena in the Dharmatā

> Three signs are associated with the exhaustion of
>   phenomena in the dharmatā:
> One's body is like a rainbow in the sky;
> One's speech repeats what others say, like an echo;
> And one's mind is like mist vanishing in the sky.

When one gains realization of the Great Perfection that transcends ordinary consciousness, physically one is like a corpse in a charnel ground, unafraid even if surrounded by a hundred executioners. Moreover, even if others' impure minds perceive one as before, from one's own yogi's point of view, one's body only appears like a rainbow in the sky. The syllables in one's channels have entered the lattice of the wisdom wind and one's speech is infused with the inexpressible, as a result of which, verbally, one repeats what others say, like an echo. And as the yogi's heart is infused with the word empowerment, their mind can, in a single instant, enter the expanse of Samantabhadra's wisdom mind endowed with six special features,[80] the primordial inner expanse, like mist that in a single instant evaporates into thin air.

iii) Nailing [Ultimate Expanse-Awareness] with the Three Kinds of Attainment

> Because one has attained mastery over outer
>   appearances,
> Everything that appears manifests as a buddha field.
> Because one has attained mastery over the illusory
>   body on the inner level,
> One's material body subsides into a pure body of
>   luminosity.
> Because one has attained mastery over wind-mind
>   on the secret level,
> When awareness is directed at the mind of an evil
>   person, that person is freed.

It is said in the *Word-Transcending Root Tantra*,

> With the three kinds of attainment that nail [ultimate
>   expanse-awareness],
> The tainted aggregates disappear.

Since one has attained mastery over outer appearances, any objects that appear are naturally purified and all appearances manifest as a buddha field. On the inner level, as one has attained mastery over the illusory body, one's material body dissolves into atoms and subsides in the state of a pure body of luminosity. On the secret level, one has attained mastery over wind-mind so that all deluded perceptions of and clinging to appearances are purified in the ultimate expanse; and by directing awareness at the mind of an evil person who has committed the five crimes with immediate retribution, one has the ability to propel that person to the level of perfect freedom.

iv) Showing the Perfect Freedom through the Four Kinds of Confident Certainty

> Four kinds of immutable great confidence apply the
> seal:
> Confidence free of the hope that one will attain
> one's goal, buddhahood;
> And confidence free of the fear that one will not
> attain it;
> Confidence free of the hope that one will cease to
> wander in samsara with its lower realms;
> And confidence free of the fear that one will
> continue wandering.

The seal applied with the four kinds of unchanging great confidence is mentioned in *Heap of Jewels*:

> With the four kinds of great confidence of the unchanging
> view,
> One cannot regress: one has seized the culmination of
> primordial wisdom.

In this life one encounters the dharmakāya, the ultimate nature of the original lord, enlightened from the beginning. One has the conviction that one's own awareness is buddha and that there is no independently existing buddha elsewhere. Consequently, one has two kinds of great confidence: one does not hope that one might attain buddhahood as one's goal, and one does not feel apprehensive that one might not attain it.

Similarly, from the point of view of primordially free and open awareness, the so-called deluded appearances of the three worlds and the six classes of beings have, from the beginning, never existed:

the three worlds are totally groundless and rootless, an unimpeded and open display devoid of location. When one realizes samsara and nirvana as the great natural openness and freedom, one has two other kinds of great confidence: one does not hope that one will cease to wander in samsara and its lower realms, and one is not fearful that one might get lost and wander there. These, then, are the four kinds of great confidence.

ii. Supplementary Instructions on the Four Bardos

These instructions comprise (1) a brief introduction and (2) a detailed explanation

A) Brief Introduction

> The ways of gaining freedom
> In the four bardos
> Are explained in brief.

Generally speaking, the explanations in texts such as *Instructions on the Six Bardos* and *Liberation by Hearing in the Bardo*[81] speak of six bardos. First, there is the teaching on the bardo of the present life, comprising the pith instruction on the natural openness and freedom of the universal ground, with the analogy of a swallow entering its nest. Second, the teaching on the bardo of dream comprises the pith instruction on the natural subsiding of delusion, with the analogy of holding up a torch in a dark room. Third, the teaching on the bardo of meditation comprises the pith instruction on the natural openness and freedom of awareness, with the analogy of an orphan finding its mother. Fourth, the teaching on the bardo of the moment of death comprises the pith instruction on one's freedom through recollection, with the analogy of a king's seal. Fifth, the teaching on the bardo of ultimate reality comprises the pith instruction on self-liberation through seeing, with the analogy of a child climbing onto its mother's lap. Sixth, the teaching on the bardo of becoming comprises the pith instruction of the analogy of connecting a broken water pipe.

Although these texts speak of six bardos, here, according to Rigdzin Jigme Lingpa's way of explaining them, there are four bardos. Thus, all the perceptions of this life, the next life, and the bardo (or of birth, death, and bardo) are here incorporated in four bardos, and the different ways of gaining freedom in them are explained in brief.

B) Detailed Explanation

The detailed explanation has four parts, dealing in turn with (1) the natural bardo, (2) the bardo of the moment of death, (3) the bardo of ultimate reality, and (4) the bardo of becoming through the ripening of karma.

1) The Natural Bardo

> First is a pith instruction for the natural bardo.
> Diligent practitioners with the greatest fortune
> Rely on the path of the teacher's profound
>   introduction
> And, in meditation and postmeditation,
> Mix the experiences of trekchö and thögal with the
>   bardo of ultimate reality.
> The luminosity of deep sleep being the luminosity of
>   dharmakāya,
> They train intensely in luminosity during the day
> And at night meditate on a five-colored sphere in
>   their heart.
> Appearances are meditated on as the nirmāṇakāya
>   buddha field of Cāmara
> And awareness as Padmasambhava.
> This is a profound pith instruction.

The natural bardo is said to correspond to the period from when one enters one's mother's womb until one is stricken by a grave, mortal illness. Here, then, is a pith instruction for the natural bardo. First of all, one enters the door of the sublime Dharma in the presence of a teacher or spiritual friend and trains progressively in listening, reflecting, and meditating. Continually immersed in faith and devotion, diligent practitioners with the greatest fortune subdue their mindstreams with the common and extraordinary teachings. After that, they attend the teacher with whom they are connected by their former aspirations and enduring karma and please him or her with the three forms of veneration. Then, relying on the profound key point of the introduction to the nature of the mind through the pith instructions of the Luminous Great Perfection, they train in the practice in four sessions, employing intense diligence, day and night. And after gaining the confidence of awareness in the trekchö practice of primordial purity, they train in the thögal practice of spontaneous presence and meditate without any distinction between formal meditation and postmeditation. They blend all the manifestations of spontaneous presence with the bardo of pure ultimate reality. And at night, in their dreams too, they begin by apprehending the luminosity of light sleep, with a limited vision of luminosity and discernment of the seen objects. Subsequently, with gradual habituation, they remain undistracted in the luminosity of deep sleep, with a vast vision of luminosity and absence of discernment of the seen objects—in other words, in the state of the luminosity of the dharmakāya. During the day, without becoming deluded, they train intensely in the continuous state of a single luminosity. And at night, they visualize a five-colored sphere comprising the five wisdoms in the middle of the heart and train in the nighttime luminosity practice. In particular, they meditate that all appearances are the Palace of Lotus Light on the Glorious Copper-Colored Mountain, the nirmāṇakāya buddha field of Cāmara, and that self-arisen awareness is Guru Padmasambhava, training repeatedly in the state of the inseparability of the teacher's mind and their own mind. All this is the profound pith instruction that has to be practiced at the time of the natural bardo.

2) The Bardo of the Moment of Death

> Second is the way of gaining freedom in the bardo of
>   the moment of death.
> In the best case, the three spaces become a single
>   state;
> Luminosity, awareness, and emptiness blend
>   inseparably into one.
> The two luminosities merge like water into water.
> In a single instant, one attains freedom in the
>   primordial ground.
> Attaining power over birth, one manifests in the
>   body of great transformation;
> Attaining power over "entering," one gains freedom
>   in the primordial inner ultimate expanse.
> Everything is freed in the secret precious dimension.
> Those with medium faculties blend consciousness
>   mounted on the wind with the dharmadhātu.
> Those with basic faculties rely on another person to
>   perform transference by joining with *A*.

The bardo of the moment of death is said to be defined as the period from the moment that one is stricken by a grave, mortal illness until the inner breath stops definitively. How one attains freedom by relying on the profound pith instructions for the time of the bardo of the moment of death is described by Jigme Lingpa as follows:

> When our time is up and we depart,
> One speaks of the bardo of the moment of death.
> At that time, may we not suffer from
> The torments and difficult circumstances of death.

By blending awareness and the ultimate expanse,
May we actually enter the sphere of luminosity
And attain freedom in the primordial ground.

If one is an individual with the highest faculties, the three spaces—
the sky that illustrates the outer space, the inner space of the empty
nature of the mind, and the secret space of the luminous essence—
coalesce in the single state of awareness. Luminosity, awareness,
and emptiness are mixed inseparably in a single taste, and the luminosity of the outer expanse and the luminosity of the inner expanse
merge like water poured into water. In a single instant one will
attain freedom in Samantabhadra's primordial ground of freedom,
as is mentioned in the *All-Illuminating Sphere Tantra*:

> When the awareness within habitual tendencies
> And the awareness dwelling in space
> Are united by means of primordial wisdom,
> One is no longer obscured by the propensities for taking
>   physical form,
> And one is freed in the great nondual state of unobstructed
>   openness.

And the *Conjunction of the Sun and Moon Tantra* states,

> Focus awareness in the eyes,
> And take the sky, for a while, as the path.
> If awareness does not waver from the ultimate expanse,
> For that person, there is no bardo:
> Buddhahood will be attained, there is no doubt.

At that time, one attains power over birth, and having manifested
in the rainbow body of great transformation, one benefits beings on
an infinite scale. Attaining power over "entering," when one wishes
to attain buddhahood, in an instant one is freed in the primordial
inner expanse. Everything is freed in the secret precious dimension

and one attains buddhahood. Subsequently, the radiance of the inner luminosity, which, though absorbed within, is not obscured, appears as outer luminosity like a face appearing in a mirror. This self-experience of awareness is the buddha field of the Dense Array, in which, within the dharmatā, the wheel of the secret, inexhaustible adornments of the enlightened body, speech, and mind, there manifest the buddhas of the five families, the half-nirmāṇakāya and half-saṃbhogakāya buddhas and others. And, until the whole of space is emptied, they benefit beings on an infinite scale. All this concerns practitioners with the highest faculties.

If one is an individual with medium faculties, one implements the instructions for the consciousness mounted on the wind using one's own resources and transfers one's consciousness through the aperture of Brahmā with the syllable *hik* and blends it with the dharmadhātu.

If one is an individual of ordinary faculties, one relies on someone else, such as one's teacher or a fellow practitioner, who joins one's consciousness to the syllable *A* and transfers it through the aperture of Brahmā.

In these two cases, the instructions for the consciousness mounted on the wind are used to transfer from the residence of samsara and enter the residence of nirvana, so we speak of "transferring from and entering a residence." Jigme Lingpa refers to these two as the bodhisattva's methods of transference.

If, at these times, transference is not possible, it is as we read in *Prayer of Aspiration for the Bardo*:[82]

> If I do not effect
> The bodhisattva's transference like that,
> As earth dissolves into earth, I cannot rise;
> As water dissolves into water, water flows from my mouth
> and nose.

Accordingly, when outwardly the four elements dissolve in stages and inwardly the experiences of light, increase of light, and full culmination of light manifest, if one recognizes these stages and remains in meditation, one is freed without necessarily losing consciousness.

3) The Bardo of Ultimate Reality

Third is the way of being freed in the bardo of
ultimate reality.
When the consciousness of the universal ground
dissolves into space,
Primordially pure luminosity appears, clear as the
autumn sky;
Having decided that it is nothing other than the
display
Of the creative power of awareness in the bardo,
And recognizing it like a child climbing onto its
mother's lap,
One attains freedom in the wisdom expanse of
Samantabhadra,
Endowed with six special features.
When space dissolves into luminosity,
The appearances of the animate and inanimate
world—
The objects outside and what perceives
them—subside,
And one's body is seen as light;
Everything that appears manifests as the five lights.
When sounds, lights, rays, and the hosts of wrathful
blood-drinking deities
And male and female buddhas of the five families,
filling space,
Dissolve into one's body, they manifest as the self-
experience of awareness.
When the state of union dissolves into primordial
wisdom,

There manifests the vision of the fourfold
  primordial wisdom,
The direct path of Vajrasattva—
Fine bands of white, yellow, red, and blue light
Connected with five round lights adorned with five
  groups of disks.
When primordial wisdom dissolves into
  spontaneous presence,
The appearances of primordial purity manifest
As the eight doors of spontaneous presence:
Awareness manifests as cognizant potency,
And as light, primordial wisdom, deities,
  nonduality,
Pure freedom from extremes, the door of impurity,
And the door of purity—primordial wisdom.
The display of the creative power of awareness
Dissolves into the ground,
And like an archer's arrow, one is free.

This presentation of how one is freed in the third bardo, the bardo of ultimate reality, needs to be examined. According to the general explanation of the bardo, the bardo of the moment of death is defined as the period from the moment one is stricken by mortal illness until the inner breath stops. It is also explained like this in *Overview of Ocean of the Single Intent: A Prayer of Aspiration for the Bardo*, composed by Khenpo Munsel Rinpoche.[83] This should mean, therefore, that the bardo of ultimate reality occurs when one recovers from having fainted and the ground luminosity manifests, and this is the case here in this text. However, in many of his writings, Omniscient Longchenpa presents liberation at the moment of death as attaining freedom at the moment that one recovers from having fainted and the ground luminosity manifests, and according to him, that is the moment when the consciousness dissolves into space. Jigme Lingpa is of the same opinion. Many other explanations of the bardo state that the moment at which the space element dissolves into luminosity is the beginning of the bardo of ultimate reality. This point, therefore, needs to be examined.

Whichever is the case, here is how freedom is attained in the bardo of ultimate reality. Once one recovers from having fainted, when the consciousness of the universal ground dissolves into space, the primordially pure ground luminosity appears, without top or bottom, periphery or center, as clear as the cloudless sky in autumn. At that time, one should decide that it is nothing other than the display of the creative power of awareness in the bardo of ultimate reality. The object of meditation, awareness as the ultimate nature (the ground luminosity that is the nature of all phenomena) is recognized by the meditating subject, awareness as the cognizant potency (the path luminosity), like a mother being recognized by her child. When one settles in meditation in this recognition, like a child climbing onto its mother's lap, one attains freedom in the wisdom expanse of Samantabhadra, which has six special features. Jigme Lingpa has written as follows:

> When I recover from having fainted and the primordial
> radiance manifests,
> Clear and unobstructed like the autumn sky,
> May I remain in that state of empty luminosity, free of
> obscuring veils.
> At that time, may I gain certainty in the wide-open, simple
> "ordinary mind" of the present moment,
> The expanse of primordial purity beyond concepts.
> And when I settle in equipoise in that state,
> May I in that very instant seize the citadel,
> The expanse of Samantabhadra's mind, endowed with six
> special features.

And in Panchen Rinpoche's *Prayer of Aspiration for the Bardo*[84] we read,

When the experience manifests free of obscurations like the
autumn sky,
Bless me that the mother and child luminosities may merge.

The six special features in this context are as follows: (1) Superiority
over the universal ground—that is, since the five lights manifest as
the wheel of spontaneous presence, we speak of them being superior to the ground. (2) Awareness experiencing itself—these five
lights are the self-experience of awareness. (3) Since the five lights
are recognized as the self-experience of awareness, and delusion and
freedom are distinguished, the particular aspects are discerned.
(4) Once confidence in this discernment is gained, buddhahood is
attained, and so freedom occurs on the basis of this discernment.
(5) Since the twenty-five aspects of the result—the primordial wisdoms, all the qualities, and so forth—are complete in awareness
itself, they do not arise through extraneous factors. And (6) since,
in fact, buddhahood's dwelling in its own place becomes manifest,
it dwells in its own place. These are the six special features of the
youthful vase body.

Now, to explain the bardo of ultimate reality in a little more
detail, the general process is that the consciousness dissolves into
space, space dissolves into luminosity, luminosity dissolves into the
state of union, the state of union dissolves into primordial wisdom,
and primordial wisdom dissolves into spontaneous presence. With
regard to consciousness dissolving into space, whether or not one
necessarily faints at the end of the three processes of light, increase
of light, and culmination of light, this is when the ground luminosity manifests. When space dissolves into luminosity, the bardo
of ultimate reality begins and all appearances [of the ground] manifest as the five lights of spontaneous presence, filling everything,
outside and inside, like an unfolded brocade.

When luminosity dissolves into the state of union, there are the
perceptions of the buddhas of the hundred families and of the triad
of sounds, lights, and shining rays. Then, over five meditation days,
there are the perceptions of the buddhas of the five families, and

awareness merges with luminosity, and luminosity merges with awareness.

When the state of union dissolves into primordial wisdom, this is the point at which the direct path of Vajrasattva manifests, with the appearances of the fourfold primordial wisdom.

When primordial wisdom dissolves into spontaneous presence, it is the stage at which the appearances of the eight doors of spontaneous presence manifest.

The first of these different stages, the dissolution of space into luminosity, is described by Jigme Lingpa as follows:

> The nature of the appearances of the ground being
>   luminosity,
> All appearances will manifest as the five lights,
> Like a brocade spread out.
> At that time, as a result of my having trained in the short
>   path of thögal,
> May I recognize them as the self-experience of awareness,
>   devoid of intrinsic existence,
> And in that instant bring them to exhaustion in ultimate
>   reality.

When consciousness dissolves into space, there arises the ground luminosity, the great primordial purity, and if one fails to recognize it, it is then time for the second stage—space dissolving into luminosity, meaning that the ground appearances, the appearances of spontaneous presence, manifest. The perceptions of objects outside (the earth, stones, mountains, and rocks) and the mind and so forth that apprehends them—in short, all the appearances of the animate and inanimate things that are perceived in this life subside and even one's own body appears as light, like a rainbow in the sky, seen or perceived as if unreal. Everything that appears or manifests arises as five-colored light, extremely bright and multihued, like an unfolded brocade, shimmering and having neither outside nor inside nor fixed dimension. It is said that at that time, for someone who has trained in the thögal practice in this life, there is the chance to attain freedom, whereas for an ordinary being, there is nothing apart from a vision like colored ribbons fluttering in the air.

At that time, in the first instant, the vision may be recognized as the self-experience of awareness. In the second, it dissolves into its nature. In the third, as soon as it dissolves, one seizes the citadel of freedom and attains buddhahood without one's needing to experience any of the subsequent visions.

If one fails to recognize this stage of space dissolving into luminosity, there occurs the third stage: luminosity dissolving into the state of union. Jigme Lingpa writes,

> As luminosity dissolves into the state of union
> And the visions of the hundred families manifest,
> If I take fright at the sounds, am scared by the rays of light
> And terrified by the sight of their bodies,
> May I know them to be a deception, like a stuffed lion,
> And achieve the confidence of fearlessness.

At this stage, space appears to be filled with sounds like a thousand thunder claps, shining lights, and piercing rays in the form of weapons, along with hosts of blood-drinking wrathful deities and peaceful deities such as the male and female buddhas of the five families—in short, the assemblies of the hundred supreme peaceful and wrathful deities. At that time, if one is frightened by the sounds, scared by the rays of light, and terrified by the sight of their bodies, one should recognize that none of these exist truly and realize that, apart from their manifesting as the self-experience of awareness, they are in truth like a fake lion made of clay. During this stage, it is said that for a period of five meditation days one will have visions of the buddhas of the five families in turn, as is found in Jigme Lingpa's writings:

> Over five meditation days,
> When I have the visions of the buddhas of the five families,

> Through the light connections between their bodies and
> myself,
> May awareness merge with luminosity,
> And through the dissolution of those bodies into me,
> May luminosity merge with awareness.
> At that time, may I attain freedom like a child climbing
> onto its mother's lap.

A "meditation day" here refers to a period of concentration—the length of time, for a practitioner meditating in the present life, between one thought ceasing and the next one arising.

On the first such day, Vairocana appears, followed by Akṣobhya, Ratnasambhava, Amitābha, Amoghasiddhi, and so on, together with their groups of deities. At these times, a fine thread of light emerges from one's heart center, connecting one to the heart of each of the buddhas of the five families. This is what we call "awareness merging with luminosity." When the deities of the five families pass down the thread of light and dissolve into one's body, manifesting as the self-experience of awareness, this is said to be "luminosity merging with awareness." At that time, if one rests in meditation with awareness focused on the path of light, one will be freed, as above. Once one is free in this manner, there is no need for the later visions to occur. This covers luminosity dissolving into the state of union.

The fourth stage is that of the state of union dissolving into primordial wisdom. When luminosity dissolves into the state of union, as has just been described, if one fails to recognize it, the state of union dissolves into the state of primordial wisdom, as we find in *Prayer of Aspiration for the Bardo*:

> As a result of the state of union dissolving
> Into primordial wisdom, there manifest lights and disks.
> Through the vision of the fourfold primordial wisdom,
> The direct path of Vajrasattva appears,
> At which point awareness seizes its natural state.

The natural radiance of the four primordial wisdoms manifests through fine bands of light, of four colors—white, yellow, red, and blue. And each of those bands of light, which are like stretched narrow rolls of cloth, are ornamented with five disks of their respective colored light. Thus, the natural radiance of the wisdom of the dharmadhātu manifests as a band of blue light, like a stretched narrow cloth, on which are five radiant disks, shining brightly like upside-down mirrors of lapis lazuli, each ornamented by five disks of their respective light. On top of that, there appears the white mirrorlike wisdom, and on top, the yellow wisdom of equality, on top of which appears the red all-perceiving wisdom. All these manifest, as above, like bands of light in their respective colors, stretched out like narrow rolls of cloth, ornamented by five respectively colored radiant disks like upturned bowls of crystal, gold, and ruby, again ornamented with five disks. These are condensed in this text as "Connected with five round lights adorned with five groups of disks." The above four bands of light are spoken of as the visions of the fourfold primordial wisdom and also as the direct path of Vajrasattva. If, when these manifest, one remembers the supreme method that is like an immutable golden scalpel and seizes the citadel of awareness, one will be freed.

The reason one speaks of the fourfold primordial wisdom while all-accomplishing wisdom is missing is that to realize all-accomplishing wisdom, one needs to accomplish deeds such as gaining stability in trekchö in this life and gaining freedom through confidence in it. If one has done so, one will have already attained freedom in this life without having to wait for the bardo of ultimate reality.

The fifth stage is that of primordial wisdom dissolving into spontaneous presence. When the state of union dissolves into primordial wisdom, as just mentioned, if one fails to recognize it, one then has to go through the dissolution of primordial wisdom into spontaneous presence. In *Prayer of Aspiration for the Bardo* we read,

As a result of primordial wisdom dissolving into
    spontaneous presence,
There will manifest the eight doors of the great primordial
    wisdom of spontaneous presence.
Deities, primordial wisdom, light disks,
Freedom from extremes, nonduality, purity and impurity,
And engaging or disengaging in samsara and nirvana
Will manifest as the self-display of awareness.
May I have confidence in primordial wisdom manifesting in
    the ground
Without moving from the ground.

The manner in which the ground appearances of primordial wisdom, primordially pure and free from elaboration, manifest as the
eight doors of spontaneous presence is as follows: (1) As a result
of the self-cognizing primordial awareness arising as cognizant
potency, compassion engages with samsara. (2) When they manifest as light, the appearance aspect of the natural light of the five
primordial wisdoms, the radiance that is present inside, shines outwardly. (3) When they manifest as primordial wisdom, since the
pure kāyas and wisdoms are none other than the self-experience
of awareness, they are, by nature, open, unimpeded emptiness. (4)
When they manifest as deities, whether they manifest as many
or few deities, they are beyond counting and are all, by nature, a
single emptiness. (5) When they manifest nondually, the deities
are present in a thought-free state of one-pointed consciousness,
where they are neither singular nor plural, neither the same nor
different. (6) When they manifest as pure freedom from extremes,
there is no extreme from which they are not free, and so they are
pristine in the very nature of awareness. (7) When they manifest
as the impure door of samsara, the whole appearance aspect of the
six classes of beings manifests distinctly and unobstructedly. And
(8) when they manifest as pure primordial wisdom, the mother and
child primordial wisdoms merge, mingling as luminosity that is

primordially pure like the cloudless autumn sky. At that time, one will have absolute confidence in this being the self-experience of awareness, as if one were meeting an old friend. As with the analogy of the immutable golden scalpel, without moving from the state of the ultimate nature, one will seize the citadel [of awareness]. And when the manifestations dissolve into the ground, one will attain freedom by settling without wavering in one's fundamental condition, like an archer's arrow that never turns back.

4) The Bardo of Becoming through the Ripening of Karma

> Fourth is the pith instruction on the bardo of
> becoming.
> All fortunate beings who meet with this profound
> teaching
> Will, by the power of truth of the ultimate nature
> and profound interdependence,
> As explained above, recognize the self-experience of
> awareness in the bardo.
> As if waking from a confused dream,
> They will take miraculous birth in the Glorious
> Mountain of Cāmara
> Or another nirmāṇakāya buddha field,
> And there they will find relief.

Here is an explanation of the pith instruction on how one attains freedom in the fourth bardo, the bardo of becoming. As we read in a tantra,

> The appearance of the body in the bardo of becoming,
> previous and future,
> Is one that has all its faculties and moves unimpededly.
> Endowed with miraculous karmic powers,
> With the pure divine eye it sees beings like itself.

"Previous" here refers to the appearance of the body one had in one's former life in the first half of the bardo, while "future" indicates the appearance of the body one will take in the next life in the last half of the bardo. The appearance of the body of becoming is not that of a coarse, substantial body but that of a mental body that one identifies with. All its faculties are complete: even if one was blind and deaf when one was alive, in this mental body all one's faculties are clear and intact. One moves unimpededly, meaning that one can pass freely without obstruction through the four elements. "Miraculous karmic powers" refers to the fact that even if one does not have the extraordinary powers that come from concentration, one has miraculous abilities that arise through karma, and in an instant one can travel round the four continents. "With the pure divine eye it sees beings like itself" means that beings in the bardo can see each other; and although, outside the bardo, they are invisible to all except those with the pure divine eye, such as spiritual masters and beings who have attained the divine eye, beings in the bardo can see the different realms of sentient beings.

Thus, although one does not have a gross body, all the faculties of a mental body are complete. Since one eats smells and burned offerings as food and is mentally related to them, one is a kind of gandharva. As one dwells between one's previous body and the next one, one is called a bardo being.[85] Of the four kinds of birth, "birth" in the bardo resembles miraculous birth as a god. Every week, one has to experience one's birth and death, so in this respect one's existence in the bardo resembles the hells. Although one is not accumulating obvious karma, one is doing so on a subtle level, and so the bardo resembles the dream state. Since one is moved by the wind of karma, one is unable to stay anywhere. As we find in *Prayer of Aspiration for the Bardo,*

> Worn out from following the wind of karma,
> Tormented by fear, every seven days
> I will experience the painful sensation of death
> And seek a place to be born.

Accordingly, all kinds of appearances manifest—the driving wind of karma, four terrifying sounds,[86] three fearful abysses,[87] six unfixed signs,[88] and so on. These are the general ways in which hallucinations manifest in the bardo. At this time, for all those who have been fortunate enough to have met with this profound teaching in the past, the power of truth of the ultimate nature and profound interdependence and the power of their having accumulated merit with their three doors in this life and of having performed a variety of positive activities are such that, as explained above, those beings will recognize all their perceptions in the bardo as being emptiness, devoid of true existence. Through the connection of profound prayers and aspirations, they will destroy the illusory machinery of all the confused appearances of the bardo, and, having destroyed them, as if waking from a dream, they will take miraculous birth in a nirmāṇakāya buddha field of luminous character such as the Glorious Mountain of Cāmara and there find relief and receive predictions. Of this there is no doubt. As Jigme Lingpa has written,

> At that time, having mentally trained in the pure fields,
> The five nirmāṇakāya buddha fields of luminous
>   character—
> Manifest Joy, Glorious,
> Piled Lotuses, Accomplishment of the Highest Activity,
> And the central Blazing Fire—
> May I, without a doubt, find freedom there.

III. Conclusion, the Virtuous Ending

The conclusion, the virtuous ending, is divided into ten parts.

A. An Instruction on the Need for Fortunate Individuals to Be Diligent in This Tantra

> This is the ultimate pith instruction: keep it in your
> heart.

Of all the different vehicles, this tantra belongs to the resultant vehicle. It is the ultimate pith instruction that enables one to attain the level of the state of union in a single life and body. And it is the profound quintessence of all the classes—the mind class, space class, and pith instruction class. Fortunate disciples and individuals who are suitable vessels should keep it in their hearts, practicing it with great perseverance and determination.

B. How, While Rejoicing, the Entourage of Disciples, the Teacher's Self-Manifestation, Were Immersed in an Expanse Where the Teacher's and Their Wisdom Minds Were Inseparable

> As the entourage of disciples,
> [The teacher's] pure self-manifestation, rejoiced,
> They were immersed in the unchanging expanse of
> realization.

With the bestowal of this Great Perfection tantra, *The Natural Openness and Freedom of the Mind*, through the mind-to-mind transmission and the subsequent rejoicing by the entourage, which is the [teacher's] pure self-manifestation, the realization of the teacher and the whole entourage blended as one taste in the unchanging dharmadhātu, thoroughly immersed in the one sole sphere of primordial purity.

C. Showing the Lineage of This Tantra

The Great Perfection teaching *The Natural*
Openness and Freedom of the Mind
Is the heart essence of the vidyādhara Garab Dorje,
Which the sublime teacher of mantras Śrīsiṃha
taught
To the son of the conquerors, Padmasambhava.
He bestowed it on his wisdom consort, the ḍākinī of
Kharchen,
Who, with the aspiration that it should benefit
beings of future generations,
Sealed it with seven immutable seals
In the precious casket of the expanse of Yudra
Nyingpo's mind.

This Great Perfection teaching *The Natural Openness and Freedom of the Mind* brings together the key points of the whole of the Buddha's teaching. It is the quintessence of all the pith instructions, the very heart of all the tantras. It is like the heart essence of the vidyādhara Garab Dorje, the great founder and charioteer of the Great Perfection. He bestowed it on the sublime teacher of the profound secret mantras, Śrīsiṃha, who gave it as an instruction to the son of the conquerors, Padmasambhava. The latter entrusted it to his wisdom consort, the lady of Kharchen, the ḍākinī Yeshe Tsogyal. The ḍākinī made inconceivable aspirations that it would benefit the beings of later generations afflicted by the five degenerations and sealed it with seven immutable seals inside the precious casket of the expanse of her disciple Yudra Nyingpo's mind.

D. An Instruction on How Extremely Profound This Tantra Is

It is the subtle essence of Padmasambhava's mind,
The very heart blood of the hundred thousand
ḍākinīs of the mother tantras,

The quintessence of omniscient Deshek Lingpa's
   treasures,
Gathering into one the teachings of the three Heart
   Essences.
It is extremely profound, the domain of the most
   fortunate beings.

This Great Perfection tantra, *The Natural Openness and Freedom
of the Mind*, is the quintessence of the subtle essence of the great
master Padmasambhava's mind. It is a profound pith instruction,
like blood that is the vital essence of the heart of the hundred thousand ḍākinīs of the mother tantras. And it is the very quintessence
of the mind treasures of the omniscient great treasure revealer
Deshek Lingpa, who is Padma's great regent. Moreover, it includes
in a single stream the teachings of the three profound Heart Essences,[89] and thus it gathers into one the treasures of the hundred
great treasure revealers. Yet compared to them, there is none more
profound than this tantra: it is extremely profound. For this reason, it lies within the scope and range of only the most fortunate
beings, ones who have already accumulated merit and made aspirations and have an enduring karmic connection.

E. Entrusting the Tantra to the Guardians of the Teaching

This profound tantra of the ultimate result
I entrust in whole to the guardians of the Great
   Perfection teachings—
The sole mother Ekajaṭī, sovereign lady of the
   mantras,
The yakṣa Shenpa Marnak,
The commander of the eight classes of spirits, and
   others.
Keep it secret from samaya breakers,
Those with wrong views, unsuitable vessels,
And others who lack fortune, intellectuals and the like.

As explained above, this resultant tantra is the ultimate essence of all the profound teachings, so the treasure revealer entrusts all the protectors of the Great Perfection teachings to guard this profound treasure—protectors such as Ekajaṭī, the sole mother of the conquerors and sovereign lady of the mantras, who has been entrusted with the six million four hundred thousand tantras of the Great Perfection; the yakṣa Shenpa Marnak, great guardian of the profound treasures; and the supreme planetary spirit Rāhula, commander-in-chief of all the eight classes of spirits. Entrusting the care of the teaching to these protectors, he tells them to keep it secret from samaya breakers, beings with wrong views, and persons who are not suitable vessels, and from beings who lack the fortune to receive such teachings, who are full of empty talk and whose approach is entirely intellectual.

F. Explaining That If One Has Wrong Views with Regard to This Profound Path, One's Downfall Will Know No Limits

> Someone who says that this does not have the
>   essence of the teachings
> Will experience the unbearable sufferings of
>   Torment Unsurpassed.

If there should perhaps be someone who criticizes this Great Perfection tantra, *The Natural Openness and Freedom of the Mind*, saying that is does not contain the essence of the teachings, that person will definitely be reborn in the hell of Torment Unsurpassed and experience the most unbearable suffering. So anyone intelligent should be careful.

G. Showing the Benefits of Practicing Properly

> All who have faith in this tantra and practice it properly—
> The protectors of virtue will constantly in this life
>   watch over them.

All living beings without exception
Who see, hear, think of it, or touch it
Will soon attain buddhahood
As the children of the conquerors.
Wherever this teaching is present,
All illnesses and misfortunes will be cleared away;
Long life, good health, and well-being
Will prevail throughout the land.
This tantra is like the wish-fulfilling jewel,
Spontaneously accomplishing the two goals.

All those who have the fortune to properly put into practice all the topics of this Great Perfection tantra, *The Natural Openness and Freedom of the Mind*, with faith and respect, will definitely, in this life, bring phenomenal appearances to exhaustion in the expanse of ultimate reality and attain freedom in the rainbow-light body. Moreover, in the meantime, even in this life, the hosts of guardians who protect virtue will stand by them and aid them in their spiritual practice. All living beings without exception who see, hear, think of, or touch this teaching will before long attain buddhahood as the children of the conquerors of the three times. Wherever this profound teaching is present, illness, negative forces, and other sources of misfortune, harm, and evil will all be cleared away. In this life people will have long lives and good health, and everything they wish for will be accomplished without effort. Throughout the land, disturbances, troubles due to disease and war, and so forth will be eliminated, and people will enjoy good fortune, happiness, and abundance and perfection. In short, this tantra is similar to the wish-fulfilling jewel that brings about everything good that one could wish for, without exception, with the power to spontaneously accomplish the two goals.

H. How This Tantra Was Drawn from a Mind Treasure

> At this present time, the very lowest point in the
> final five hundred years,
> When the essential teachings are drifting toward
> Varuṇa the water god,
> In order to bring fortunate beings of future
> generations to maturity,
> I drew this from the casket of the unchanging
> dharmakāya of my mind.

At the present time, when we are at the very lowest point in the final five-hundred-year period and people are wearied and oppressed by the troubles of these bad times, the sun of the essential teachings and pith instructions is moving in the direction of Varuṇa the water god in the west and about to set. At this time, in order to bring to maturity the mindstreams of fortunate disciples in future generations and free them, the great treasurer revealer Deshek Lingpa withdrew this ultimate tantra from the casket of the unchanging dharmakāya, the secret treasure of his mind.

I. A Concluding Prayer of Aspiration

> For as long as space endures, may this precious king
> of tantras
> Fully remain for the benefit of infinite sentient
> beings,
> And may they all be completely freed within the
> precious secret,
> The dharmakāya that is doubly pure.

For as long as space endures, may this king of tantras, the precious Great Perfection teaching, *The Natural Openness and Freedom of the Mind*, be placed on the apex of the victory banner without its ever being lowered. May its activity as a protector and ally for infinite sentient beings remain unimpaired, and may limitless beings all attain nondwelling complete freedom within the precious secret expanse, the wisdom mind of the primordially pure dharmakāya endowed with the two purities.[90]

J. Applying the Seal of Secrecy and Indicating That the Text Is Complete and Concluded

> Samaya. Sealed, sealed, sealed.
> This completes the text titled *The Great Perfection Tantra, The Natural Openness and Freedom of the Mind.*

"Samaya" signifies entrusting the secret profound words to disciples with good fortune who keep the sacred commitments (*samayas*). "Sealed, sealed, sealed" signifies placing outer, inner, and secret seals on the teaching so that it is not leaked at any time—even spoken in the wind that blows in the direction of those who have broken the samaya and harbor wrong views.

Then, to show that the main body of the text has been completed and is now concluded, this verse properly completes, with its beginning, middle, and end, the text known as the king of tantras, a pith instruction on the natural openness and freedom of the mind itself, the primordial secret of the wisdom of the Natural Great Perfection.

Concluding Poem

As a result of having accumulated merit over numerous kalpas,
I have gained the opportunity to explain the meaning of this tantra,
And even though I am now feeble-minded and burdened by the
    years,
I am filled with joy, thinking, "How lucky I am!"

Yet it is difficult for someone like me to understand it fully,
Simple as I am and bereft of the qualities of having trained in this
    life.
So, all the mistakes I have made—contradictions, non sequiturs,
    and so on—
I confess before the three roots and lords and guardians of the
    treasure.

By the merit of the efforts I have made in this, may all beings
Be freed from the shell of dualistic ignorance
And, realizing their own awareness, dharmakāya,
Find freedom in the primordial ground, the inner space.

Colophon

The great treasure revealer, the king of Dharma, appointed me as
the holder of this profound teaching and gave me many auspicious
materials, saying, "You should also write a commentary on it."
Unable to go against this command that he had honored me with,
I, Tenpa'i Wangchuk, bearing the incarnation name Khangsar,
wrote this commentary on *The Great Perfection Tantra, The Natural Openness and Freedom of the Mind*, titled *The Light of Wisdom*.

Virtue! Virtue! Virtue! Mangalaṃ

PART THREE

A Key for Opening the Treasury of Instructions of the Three Lineages

A Structural Analysis of
The Great Perfection Tantra,
The Natural Openness and
Freedom of the Mind

The text called *The Great Perfection Tantra, The Natural Openness and Freedom of the Mind* is the quintessence of the six million four hundred thousand tantras of the Great Perfection, bringing together the essential points of the seventeen tantras of the Heart Essence, a profound teaching that appeared as a mind treasure of the great treasure revealer, Deshek Lingpa. It is a pith instruction more precious than the eyes in one's forehead or the blood in one's heart. It is this text, which is like the excellent wish-fulfilling jewel, that will be explained here.

The explanation is divided into three sections: (1) a virtuous beginning, the introduction; (2) a virtuous middle, the text itself; and (3) a virtuous ending, the conclusion. The first of these has two parts: (1) the meaning of the title and (2) the homage.

I. Introduction, the virtuous beginning

A. Title (In Sanskrit: *Mahāsandhyacittasvamuktatantranama*)

B. Homage (Homage to the primordial lord!)

II. The text itself, the virtuous middle

A. Preliminaries

1. The setting

a. Brief outline (In the sublime place free of limits and beyond extremes . . .)

b. Detailed explanation (This tantra of the ultimate result . . .)

2. The manner in which the key points of the infinite tantras are included within this tantra (It is the essence of the profound key points . . .)

3. Showing that this tantra is the essence of all the different teachings of the buddhas (The profound key points . . .)

4. Showing that this tantra is the sole path trodden by the buddhas past, present, and future (This is the sole path trodden by all . . .)

5. Showing how this tantra outshines all the intellectual philosophical tenet systems of the eight vehicles (It will not be realized . . .)

B. Main practice

1. Brief outline (The unborn ground expanse . . .)

2. Detailed explanation

a. The practice of primordial purity, trekchö—the path by which lazy persons gain freedom without effort

i. Establishing the view of the ground

A) A general description of the practices accessory to the view

1) An explanation of the distinction between samsara and nirvana, freedom and delusion

a) A presentation of the original common ground (In the beginning . . .)

b) How the appearances of spontaneous presence unfold (When, with the movement . . .)

c) How, when one recognizes one's own nature, one is freed directly within the primordial ground (The instant the appearances . . .)

d) How, when one fails to recognize one's own nature, one is deluded and thus wanders in samsara (Failing to recognize . . .)

2) Showing how it is necessary to train in whichever of the four yogas is appropriate, depending on the dispositions and faculties of the disciples (For someone who . . .)

3) The outer rushen separation practice for the three doors (Next, in the rushen separation practice . . .)

    a) Separation practice related to the body

    b) Separation practice related to speech

    c) Separation practice related to mind

4) The inner purification by burning up the seeds of the six realms (Inwardly, in the crown . . .)

5) The guiding instructions in terms of the ordinary mind, showing the methods for purifying the three doors (To purify the body . . .)

    a) Purification of the body

    b) Purification of speech

        i) Placing the seal

           (A) Placing the seal on outer appearances

           (B) Placing the seal on one's own body

        ii) Developing the technique

           (A) Developing the technique with regard to outer appearances

           (B) Developing the technique with regard to one's body

        iii) Achieving mental suppleness

        iv) Journeying on the road

c) Purification of the mind

6) Relaxing the three doors in their natural state (One should relax . . .)

7) Examining which, of the body, speech, and mind, is the most important (One should examine . . .)

8) Looking for where the mind comes from, dwells, and goes (One should investigate . . .)

9) Distinguishing mind and awareness (The universal ground . . .)

B) A specific explanation of the main practice, the introduction to the nature of awareness

1) Showing the fundamental nature of awareness

a) Differences between the relative and ultimate and distinctions between knowledge and ignorance (Genuine awareness . . .)

b) Introducing awareness that is the three kāyas, free of thoughts related to the three times (When one leaves . . .)

c) Showing that awareness, luminous and empty, free of clinging, is the one and only sphere (Empty luminosity . . .)

d) Introducing inexpressible awareness, the fourth state in which the other three are absent (Genuine awareness, the fourth state . . .)

e) Introducing the great natural openness and freedom of awareness that is free of all assertions (Ineffable, inconceivable . . .)

f) Introducing the great equality of awareness, appearance and emptiness inseparable (All the phenomena . . .)

2) Showing the means for making awareness manifest

a) Showing how awareness is made manifest when one settles naturally in the state devoid of something to be seen and someone who sees (Potentially either buddha . . .)

b) Explaining how, if one relies on effortful meditation practice, one will not see the fundamental nature beyond meditation (It transcends . . .)

c) How the way of being of samsara and nirvana becomes manifest clearly and distinctly (When the sun . . .)

d) Distilling all the appearances of samsara and nirvana into the single, primordially pure awareness (Though the appearing . . .)

e) Showing that all the phenomena of samsara and nirvana are of one taste in awareness, the state of the great equality (Appearances are equal . . .)

ii. How to preserve the true nature of awareness by practicing the path of nonmeditation (When one encounters . . .)

iii. An explanation of the conduct that accords with the natural openness and freedom of the mind and accompanies the view and meditation

A) The main teaching on the conduct that accords with the natural openness and freedom of the mind (When one has gained . . .)

B) A supplementary explanation on avoiding the dangers of deviations, errors, and mistakes (Whatever meditative experiences . . .)

iv. How the twenty-five aspects of the result are inherently complete in awareness (As for the twenty-five . . .)

b. The practice of spontaneous presence, thögal—by which diligent persons gain freedom through effort

  i. The main explanation of thögal

    A) Brief introduction (The direct path . . .)

    B) Detailed explanation

      1) A general explanation (From the moment . . .)

      2) A specific explanation of the different divisions of thögal

        a) How, relying on skillful means, the four lamps are made manifest

          i) How one relinquishes the nine activities of the three doors (First, the nine activities . . .)

          ii) Relying on four crucial points as the method for making manifest the four lamps (It is in dependence on four . . .)

          iii) How the vision of the four lamps arises as cause and result (The lamp of the empty disks . . .)

          iv) How the four lamps make it possible for the luminous appearances to unfold (How do the four lamps . . .)

          v) The main explanation of the four lamps

(A) An explanation of the precious heart (In the hollow . . .)

(B) The lamp of the smooth, white channel (The pure channel . . .)

(C) The lamp of the far-catching water lasso (In the pupils . . .)

(D) The lamp of the utterly pure ultimate expanse (When one looks . . .)

(E) The lamp of the empty disks of light (Within the lamp . . .)

(F) The lamp of self-arisen wisdom (Inner awareness . . .)

(G) The chains of awareness (Within it, there appear . . .)

(H) A supplementary explanation of a few points of interest (The contributory factors . . .)

b) How one progresses through the four visions of thögal

i) Brief introduction (With the lamp . . .)

ii) Detailed explanation

(A) The vision of the dharmatā in reality (One realizes the four . . .)

(B) The vision of the enhanced experiences of awareness (Circular disks . . .)

(C) The vision of the climax of awareness (In the center . . .)

(D) The vision of the exhaustion of phenomena in the dharmatā (All appearances . . .)

c) Four supporting pith instructions

i) Laying the foundation with the three kinds of motionlessness (Then there are the supporting instructions . . .)

ii) Grasping the extent [of stability] with the three kinds of settling

    (A) The main explanation (The extent of [stability]. . .)

    (B) Incidental points

        (1) Dreams (As for grasping the extent . . .)

        (2) Signs

            (a) Brief introduction (The signs of proficiency . . .)

            (b) Detailed explanation

                (i) The three signs associated with the dharmatā in reality (Three signs are associated with the vision . . .)

                (ii) The three signs associated with the enhanced experiences of awareness (Three signs are associated with the enhanced experiences . . .)

                (iii) The three signs associated with the climax of awareness (Three signs are associated with the climax . . .)

                (iv) The three signs associated with the exhaustion of phenomena in the dharmatā (Three signs are associated with the exhaustion . . .)

iii) Nailing [ultimate expanse-awareness] with the three kinds of attainment (Because one has attained . . .)

iv) Showing the perfect freedom through the four kinds of confident certainty (Four kinds of immutable . . .)

ii. Supplementary instructions on the four bardos

   A) Brief introduction (The ways of gaining freedom . . .)

   B) Detailed explanation

      1) The natural bardo (First is a pith instruction . . .)

      2) The bardo of the moment of death (Second is the way of gaining freedom . . .)

      3) The bardo of ultimate reality (Third is the way of being freed . . .)

      4) The bardo of becoming through the ripening of karma (Fourth is the pith instruction . . .)

III. Conclusion, the virtuous ending

A. An instruction on the need for fortunate individuals to be diligent in this tantra (This is the ultimate . . .)

B. How, while rejoicing, the entourage of disciples, the teacher's self-manifestation, were immersed in an expanse where the teacher's and their wisdom minds were inseparable (As the entourage of disciples . . .)

C. Showing the lineage of this tantra (The Great Perfection teaching . . .)

D. An instruction on how extremely profound this tantra is (It is the subtle essence . . .)

E. Entrusting the tantra to the guardians of the teaching (This profound tantra . . .)

F. Explaining that if one has wrong views with regard to this profound path, one's downfall will know no limits (Someone who says . . .)

G. Showing the benefits of practicing properly (All who have faith . . .)

H. How this tantra was drawn from a mind treasure (At this present time . . .)

I. A concluding prayer of aspiration (For as long as space . . .)

J. Applying the seal of secrecy and indicating that the text is complete and concluded (Samaya. Sealed . . .)

Written by one who bears the name Tenpa.

Virtue!

NOTES

ABBREVIATIONS

TPQ, Book 2 Jigme Lingpa and Longchen Yeshe Dorje, Kangyur Rinpoche. *Treasury of Precious Qualities, Book 2: Vajrayana and the Great Perfection.* Translated by the Padmakara Translation Group. Boston: Shambhala, 2013.

TFN Longchenpa and Khangsar Tenpa'i Wangchuk. *The Precious Treasury of the Fundamental Nature.* Translated by the Padmakara Translation Group. Boulder: Shambhala, 2021.

1. The composition of written commentaries by scholars other than Longchenpa himself is a feature of recent decades and no doubt reflects the perceived dangers to the tradition that recent persecution has rendered so fragile. In this respect, the commentaries by Tenpa'i Wangchuk are, happily, not unique. His contemporary, Khenpo Jamyang Drubpa'i Lodrö of Domang, composed a full-length word commentary on *The Precious Treasury of Pith Instructions* (*Man ngag rin po che'i mdzod*). Of course, the word-of-mouth transmission of Longchenpa's writings has been maintained unbroken down the centuries, and thanks to modern technology, attempts have been made in recent years to transcribe and translate the oral explanations of living teachers, notably the very detailed commentary on Longchenpa's *Precious Treasury of Pith Instructions* given by Dilgo Khyentse Rinpoche in Bhutan in 1985.

2. Deshek Lingpa (1956–2020) is also known as Tulku Lhatsam and Tertön Padma Jigme Dorje, the abbot of Dogongma Monastery and Dogabma Monastery (founded by Dudjom Lingpa). He used the name Deshek Lingpa after his previous incarnation as Gompa Tertön Chökyi Dorje, who was a student of Dudjom Lingpa.

3. Pronounced "ṇi" by Tibetans.

4. Kumbhāṇḍas are a type of spirit with animal heads and human bodies.

5. *kun mkhyen yab sras,* referring to Kunkhyen Longchenpa and Kunkhyen Jigme Lingpa.

6. *gter chen bde gshegs gling pa'i dgongs gter las byon pa*, literally "appeared from the treasury of the great treasure revealer Deshek Lingpa's wisdom mind."

7. Of the three kinds of homage—physically performing prostrations and so on, vocally singing praises, and mentally "meeting with the view"—this last is the supreme homage.

8. This third part in fact refers to the virtuous ending and not to a third section within the virtuous middle.

9. The different kāyas, or buddha bodies, mentioned here follow the classification of the three kāyas into nine, the dharmakāya (body of ultimate reality) being divided into the dharmakāya aspect of the dharmakāya, saṃbhogakāya aspect of the dharmakāya, and nirmāṇakāya aspect of the dharmakāya. The saṃbhogakāya (body of perfect enjoyment) is similarly divided into the dharmakāya aspect of the saṃbhogakāya, saṃbhogakāya aspect of the saṃbhogakāya, and so on, and likewise the nirmāṇakāya (body of manifestation).

10. *Guhyagarbha Tantra* (*gSang ba'i snying po de kho na nyid nges pa*).

11. Longchenpa, *Treasury of the Dharmadhātu*, ch. 13, v. 3b.

12. Longchenpa, *Treasury of the Dharmadhātu*, ch. 13, v. 3c.

13. *yid can*, practitioners who consider that phenomena are not different from the nature of the mind. See *TPQ, Book 2*, 254.

14. Longchenpa, *Treasury of the Dharmadhātu*, ch. 7, v. 2.

15. For a detailed presentation of the different sections mentioned here, see pp. 192–94.

16. For the five states, see Longchenpa, *Finding Rest in the Nature of the Mind*, translated by the Padmakara Translation Group (Boulder: Shambhala, 2017), 276n61.

17. *nang gsal thum la rmugs bral*. See Longchenpa, *Finding Rest*, 295n135, and *TPQ, Book 2*, 438n457.

18. For the eight doors of spontaneous presence, see below, pp. 177–78.

19. The use here of the pronoun "he" is merely a convention. At the level of Samantabhadra, there is of course no concept of "he" or "she" or even "Samantabhadra."

20. *TPQ, Book 2*, ch. 11, v. 22.

21. "Separation" refers to the separation of samsara and nirvana (*'khor 'das ru shan*).

22. See part one, note 4.

23. Pronounced "ṇi" by Tibetans.

24. Literally "press your Adam's apple down" (*mgrin pas ol mdud non par byas*).

25. Drime Özer is another of Omniscient Longchenpa's names.

26. See *TPQ, Book 2*, 135.

27. *mtho gang*, the span from the tip of the thumb to the tip of the middle finger.

28. Some texts speak of these two practices—relaxing in the natural state (*rnal du dbab*) and refreshing oneself (*sor gzhug*)—separately.

29. *dbyibs brgyad*. The traditional shapes are long, short, square, round, tall (high), short (low), smooth, and irregular.

30. The primary colors (*rtsa ba'i kha dog*) in this context are blue, white, yellow, red, and green. The eight secondary tones, or color modifiers (*yan lag gi kha dog brgyad po*), are cloud, smoke, dust, haze, sunlight, shade, light, and dark.

31. *O rgyan chen po*. The name by which Guru Padmasambhava is known, after his birthplace.

32. "Truly existent" implies a self that is a single, permanent, and independent entity.

33. See p. 194.

34. *rig dang ma rig*. Although *rig pa* has usually been rendered in this translation as "awareness," in this context, as the opposite of ignorance (*ma rig pa*), we have chosen to render *rig pa* as "knowledge." An alternative translation of this phrase would be "awareness and lack of awareness."

35. See note 34.

36. *TFN*, "Single Nature," v. 1.

37. As mentioned on p. 88, the three blemishes (*skyon gsum*) appear to be dust, wind, and clouds.

38. *TFN*, "Spontaneous Presence," v. 4.

39. Longchenpa, *Treasury of the Dharmadhātu*, ch. 2, v. 11.

40. Longchenpa, *Treasury of the Dharmadhātu*, ch. 1, v. 1.

41. *TFN*, "Evenness," v. 9.

42. *The Way of the Bodhisattva*, trans. Padmakara Translation Group, r. ed. (Boston: Shambhala, 2006), 137.

43. See the glossary for Tibetan equivalents of these terms.

44. Also known as Langdro Lotsāwa, one of Guru Padmasambhava's twenty-five disciples.

45. Despite the author's attribution of this quotation to *The Treasury of the Fundamental Nature*, we have been unable to locate it in that text or elsewhere.

46. Tenpa'i Wangchuk quotes this passage without these two lines in the original text.

47. *TFN*, "Single Nature," v. 2.

48. Longchenpa, *Treasury of the Dharmadhātu*, ch. 3, vv. 9–10.

49. Longchenpa, *Treasury of the Dharmadhātu*, ch. 8, v. 3.

50. Longchenpa, *Treasury of the Dharmadhātu*, ch. 4, v. 1.

51. *The Cloudless Sky* (*Nam mkha' sprin bral*) is an instruction text on the practice of trekchö by Tenpa'i Wangchuk's teacher Lodrö Gyatso on which Tenpa'i Wangchuk wrote a commentary, included in his Collected Works.

52. *'khor gsum*; subject, object, and action.

53. *TFN*, "Single Nature," v. 1.

54. *TFN*, "Single Nature," v. 1.

55. Longchenpa, *Treasury of the Dharmadhātu*, ch. 10, v. 4.

56. Longchenpa, *Treasury of the Dharmadhātu*, ch. 2, v. 4 (last two lines) and v. 5 (first three lines).

57. *TFN*, "Nonexistence," v. 24.

58. That is, a cloudless, windless, dustless sky.

59. See *TPQ, Book 2*, 398n238.

60. Longchenpa, *Treasury of the Dharmadhātu*, ch. 10, v. 7.4.

61. *sku lnga*; the five kinds of enlightened body.

62. *mngon par byang chub pa'i sku*; the body of manifest enlightenment. For the five kāyas, see also Jamgön Kongtrul, *The Treasury of Knowledge: Journey and Goal, Books 9 and 10*, translated by Kalu Rinpoché Translation Group (Ithaca, NY: Snow Lion, 2011), 415–16.

63. Although the Tibetan here reads *grags pa gnyis su med pa*, we have followed an almost identical rendering in Jamgön Kongtrul's *Treasury of Knowledge* (*Shes bya kun khyab mdzod*) that reads *grags stong gnyis su med pa*.

64. According to Jamgön Kongtrul's *Treasury of Knowledge*, the quotations in this description of the five qualities are taken from the *Guhyagarbha Tantra*. See Jamgön Kongtrul, *The Treasury of Knowledge: Journey and Goal, Books 9 and 10*, 418 and 633nn1012–1016.

65. Other versions of this quotation have *mnyen* (flexible or gentle) instead of *mnyam* (literally "equal"), which would read in translation, "Those whose minds are filled with defiled thoughts / Are made gentle and peaceful by the buddhas' deeds."

66. The example is given of a snail's horns. If one touches one, it retracts while the other is stretched out. Similarly, when the pure channels are "working," the impure channels work less, and vice versa.

67. The phrase "root tantra" (*rtsa rgyud*) refers to the *Word-Transcending Root Tantra* (*sGra thal 'gyur rtsa ba'i rgyud*) again.

68. *tsitta sha'i sgron ma.*
69. *citta zur brgyad pho brang.*
70. *ba men*; the gaur or Indian bison, which has large curved horns.
71. *gra zur las 'das pa*; completely devoid of angles and corners (meaning, they are not square or triangular).
72. The Tibetan term *thig le* has a number of different translations that depend on the context: "disk," "sphere," or "essence-drop."
73. *'og min*; the buddha field called The Unexcelled.
74. Although Tenpa'i Wangchuk attributes this quotation to Shabkar Tsokdruk Rangdröl's *Flight of the Garuda* (*mKha' lding gshog rlabs*), it is actually located in another text by the same author, *Excellent Vase of Nectar: A Song of Oral Advice on the Key Points of Thögal* (*Thod rgal gnad kyi zhal shes mgur dbyangs bdud rtsi'i bum bzang zhes bya ba*).
75. Lights that can be used for thögal practice include lamps with a flame and old-fashioned clear electric light bulbs with a glowing filament.
76. *rang bzhin sprul sku.* See *TPQ, Book 2*, 242 et seq.
77. The vowel sign *naro:* ⌣
78. See *TPQ, Book 2*, 294 et seq.
79. *mkha' 'gro'am bya 'dab chags*; literally "sky-goer or bird or feathered creature."
80. For the six special features, see p. 172.
81. *drug khrid* and *thos grol*; referring to the treasures of Karma Lingpa.
82. Jigme Lingpa, *Bar do'i smon lam dgongs gcig rgya mtsho.*
83. *Bar do'i smon lam dgongs gcig rgya mtsho'i spyi don*, an overview of Jigme Lingpa's prayer, composed by Khenpo Munsel Tsultrim Gyatso (1916–1993).
84. We have not been able to locate this work or identify its author.
85. *bar do ba*, "a being in between."
86. The four terrifying sounds (*'jigs pa'i sgra bzhi*) are the sound of an avalanche or earthquake, the roar of the waves, a forest fire, and a hurricane, with the perceptions of being crushed under the earth, swept away by water, burned by fire, and blown away by the wind.
87. The three fearful abysses (*ya nga ba'i g.yang gsum*) refer to the experiences of falling into extremely frightening ravines that are white, red, or black (related to the three poisons—attachment, aversion, and ignorance).
88. The six unfixed signs (*ma nges pa'i rtags drug*) refer to fleeting experiences that indicate that one is in the bardo. They concern the unfixed, short-lived experiences of the place (mountain peaks, empty plains, uninhabited buildings, etc.), support (roads, stūpas, etc.), behavior (a variety of

different actions), food (the different foods of the six classes of beings, which even if one sees them, one cannot eat), company (pleasant and unpleasant companions, different bardo beings, gods and spirits, etc.), and mental impressions (pleasure and pain, etc.).

89. *snying thig rnam gsum*; the Heart Essence teachings of Vimalamitra, Padmasambhava, and Vairotsana.

90. The two purities (*dag pa gnyis*) are original purity (*rang bzhin ye dag*), which is the buddha nature in all beings, and purity from all adventitious stains (*blo bur phral dag*).

GLOSSARY

awake	*hrig ge*
awareness	*rig pa*
character (luminous)	*rang bzhin*
cognizant power/potency	*thugs rje*
creative power	*rtsal*
display	*rol ba*
equality	*mnyam nyid*
evenness	*phyal ba*
fundamental condition	*gshis*
fundamental nature	*gnas lugs*
gain clear conviction (to)	*la bzla ba*
hallucinatory appearances	*'khrul snang*
hazy	*bun ne*
luminosity	*'od gsal*
mind's subjective experience	*rang snang*
naked	*rjen ne*
natural openness and freedom	*rang grol*
nature (ultimate)	*ngo bo*
nonexistence	*med pa*
nonreferential	*yul med*
not torpid	*phyal min*
open and unimpeded	*zang thal*
open(ness) and free(dom)	*grol ba*
ornament	*rgyan*
peaceful	*khris se*

pellucid	*sal le*
primordial/primal wisdom	*ye shes*
pure	*yer re*
self-cognizing primordial wisdom	*(rang) rig pa'i ye shes*
self-experience (of awareness)	*(rig pa'i) rang snang*
spontaneous presence	*lhun grub*
spontaneously present	*lhun gyis grub pa*
subside (to)	*grol ba*
ultimate reality, dharmatā	*chos nyid*
unclouded	*rdul bral*
vivid	*wal le*

Texts Cited in Khangsar Tenpa'i Wangchuk's Commentary

All-Illuminating Sphere Tantra, *Thig le kun gsal gyi rgyud*
Array of Studded Jewels Tantra, *Nor bu phra bkod*
Conjunction of the Sun and Moon Tantra, *Nyi zla kha sbyor gyi rgyud*
Diamond Cutter Sūtra, *rDo rje gcod pa, Vajracchedikā*
Distinguishing Three Key Points, *gNad gsum shan 'byed* by Kunkhyen
    Jigme Lingpa
Flight of the Garuḍa, *mKha' lding gshog rlabs* by Shabkar Tsokdruk Rangdröl
Golden Garland, *gSer phreng*
Heap of Jewels Tantra, *Rin po che spungs pa'i rgyud*
Heart Essence of Vairotsana, *Bai ro'i thugs thig*
Highest Wisdom, *Khrid yig ye shes bla ma* by Kunkhyen Jigme Lingpa
Later Tantra of the Expanse of Samantabhadra's Wisdom, *Kun tu bzang po
    ye shes klong gi rgyud phyi ma*
Later Tantra of the Heart Essence, *sNying thig gi rgyud phyi ma*
Luminous Expanse, *kLong gsal gyi rgyud*
Mirror of Samantabhadra's Mind, *Kun tu bzang po'i thugs kyi me long*
Necklace of Pearls Tantra, *Mu tig 'phreng ba'i rgyud, Muktāvali*
Net of Illusory Manifestations Tantra, *sGyu 'phrul drva ba'i rgyud,
    Māyājālatantra*
Only Child of the Buddhas, *Sangs rgyas sras gcig*
Only Child of the Teaching Tantra, *bsTan pa bu gcig gi rgyud*
Prayer of Aspiration for the Bardo, *Bar do'i smon lam* by "Panchen Rin-
    poche" (unidentified)
Prayer of Aspiration for the Bardo, *Bar do'i smon lam dgongs gcig rgya mtsho*
    by Kunkhyen Jigme Lingpa
Refutation of Criticisms, *rTsod pa bzlog pa, Vigrahavyāvartanīkārikā* by
    Nāgārjuna
Self-Illuminating Awareness, *Rig pa rang gsal (Chos thams cad kyi don ston
    pa rdzogs chen thig le nyag gcig ye nas bya rtsal bral ba)*

Stainless Tantra of Mañjuśrī, *'Jam dpal dri ma med pa'i rgyud*

Sun, Moon, Planets, and Stars, *Nyi zla gza' skar*

Tantra Fragment "Stirring the Depths," *Dong sprugs bkol ba dum bu'i rgyud*

Tantra of Awareness Self-Arisen, *Rig pa rang shar gyi rgyud*

Tantra of Samantabhadra, *Kun tu bzang po'i rgyud*

Tantra of the All-Creating King, *Kun byed rgyal po'i rgyud*

Tantra of the Blazing Relics, *sKu gdung 'bar ba'i rgyud*

Tantra of the Expanse of Samantabhadra's Wisdom, *Kun tu bzang po ye shes klong gi rgyud*

Tantra of the Secret Word, *gSang ba sgra rgyud*

Tantra of the Self-Arising Fundamental Nature, *gNas lugs rang byung gi rgyud*

Testament, *'Das rjes ('Od gsal rdzogs pa chen po man ngag sde'i gnad kyi bcud phud sangs rgyas kyi 'das rjes gsum)*

The Cloudless Sky, *Khregs chod kyi khrid yig nam mkha' sprin bral* by Lodrö Gyatso

The Precious Treasury of the Dharmadhātu, *Chos dbyings mdzod* by Kunkhyen Longchenpa

The Precious Treasury of the Fundamental Nature, *gNas lugs mdzod* by Kunkhyen Longchenpa

The Treasury of Words and Meanings, *Tshig don mdzod* by Kunkhyen Longchenpa

Unwritten Tantra, *Yi ge med pa'i rgyud*

Vajra Verses on the Fundamental Nature, *gNas lugs rdo rje'i tshig rkang*

Word-Transcending Root Tantra, *sGra thal 'gyur rtsa ba'i rgyud*

BIBLIOGRAPHY

Jamgön Kongtrul Lodrö Taye. "The Heart Essence Mother and Child." In *Nyingma, Part Two.* Vol. 2 of The Treasury of Precious Instructions. Translated by the Padmakara Translation Group. Boulder: Snow Lion, 2024.

———. *The Treasury of Knowledge: Journey and Goal, Books 9 and 10.* Translated by Kalu Rinpoché Translation Group. Ithaca, NY: Snow Lion, 2011

Jigme Lingpa and Longchen Yeshe Dorje, Kangyur Rinpoche. *Treasury of Precious Qualities, Book 2: Vajrayana and the Great Perfection.* Translated by the Padmakara Translation Group. Boston: Shambhala, 2013.

Khangsar Tenpa'i Wangchuk. *Chos dbyings rin po che'i mdzod kyi 'bru 'grel 'od gsal thig le nyag gcig ces bya ba.* Khang sar bstan pa'i dbang phyug gi gsung 'bum, vol. 5. Beijing: Mi rigs dpe skrun khang, 2005.

———. *rDzogs pa chen po sems nyid rang grol gyi rgyud kyi 'grel pa ye shes 'od snang zhes bya ba.* Khang sar bstan pa'i dbang phyug gi gsung 'bum, vol. 4. Beijing: Mi rigs dpe skrun khang, 2005.

Longchenpa. *Finding Rest in the Nature of the Mind.* Translated by the Padmakara Translation Group. Boulder: Shambhala, 2017.

Longchenpa and Khangsar Tenpa'i Wangchuk. *The Precious Treasury of the Fundamental Nature.* Khangsar Tenpa'i Wangchuk's Collected Works. Translated by the Padmakara Translation Group. Boulder, Shambhala, 2021.

THE PADMAKARA TRANSLATION GROUP
TRANSLATIONS INTO ENGLISH

The Adornment of the Middle Way. Shantarakshita and Mipham Rinpoche. Boston: Shambhala, 2005, 2010.

A Chariot to Freedom. Shechen Gyaltsap. Boulder: Shambhala, 2021.

Counsels from My Heart. Dudjom Rinpoche. Boston: Shambhala, 2001, 2003.

Enlightened Courage. Dilgo Khyentse Rinpoche. Dordogne: Editions Padmakara, 1992; Ithaca, NY: Snow Lion, 1994, 2006.

The Excellent Path of Enlightenment. Dilgo Khyentse. Dordogne: Editions Padmakara, 1987; Ithaca, NY: Snow Lion, 1996.

A Feast of the Nectar of the Supreme Vehicle. Jamgön Mipham. Boulder: Shambhala, 2018.

Finding Rest in Meditation. Longchenpa. Boulder: Shambhala, 2018.

Finding Rest in the Nature of the Mind. Longchenpa. Boulder: Shambhala, 2017.

Finding Rest in Illusion. Longchenpa. Boulder: Shambhala, 2017.

A Flash of Lightning in the Dark of Night. The Dalai Lama. Boston: Shambhala, 1993. Republished as *For the Benefit of All Beings.* Boston: Shambhala, 2009.

Food of Bodhisattvas. Shabkar Tsogdruk Rangdrol. Boston: Shambhala, 2004.

A Garland of Views: A Guide to View, Meditation, and Result in the Nine Vehicles. Padmasambhava and Mipham Rinpoche. Boston: Shambhala, 2015.

A Guide to the Words of My Perfect Teacher. Khenpo Ngawang Pelzang. Translated with Dipamkara. Boston: Shambhala, 2004.

The Heart of Compassion. Dilgo Khyentse. Boston: Shambhala, 2007.

The Heart Treasure of the Enlightened Ones. Dilgo Khyentse and Patrul Rinpoche. Boston: Shambhala, 1992.

The Hundred Verses of Advice. Dilgo Khyentse and Padampa Sangye. Boston: Shambhala, 2005.

Introduction to the Middle Way. Chandrakirti and Mipham Rinpoche. Boston: Shambhala, 2002, 2004.

Journey to Enlightenment. Matthieu Ricard. New York: Aperture Foundation, 1996.

Lady of the Lotus-Born. Gyalwa Changchub and Namkhai Nyingpo. Boston: Shambhala, 1999, 2002.

The Life of Shabkar: The Autobiography of a Tibetan Yogin. Albany, NY: SUNY Press, 1994. Reprinted in Ithaca, NY: Snow Lion, 2001.

Mahāsiddha Practice. The Treasury of Precious Instructions, vol. 16. Jamgön Kongtrul. Boulder: Snow Lion, 2021.

Nagarjuna's Letter to a Friend. Longchen Yeshe Dorje, Kangyur Rinpoche. Ithaca, NY: Snow Lion, 2005, 2013.

The Nectar of Manjushri's Speech. Kunzang Pelden. Boston: Shambhala, 2007.

Nyingma, Part Two. The Treasury of Precious Instructions, vol. 2. Jamgön Kongtrul. Boulder: Snow Lion, 2024.

The Precious Treasury of the Fundamental Nature. Longchenpa and Khangsar Tenpa'i Wangchuk. Khangsar Tenpa'i Wangchuk's Collected Works. Boulder: Shambhala, 2021.

Practicing the Great Perfection: Instructions on the Crucial Points. Shechen Gyaltsap Gyurmé Pema Namgyal. Boulder: Shambhala, 2020.

The Root Stanzas on the Middle Way. Nāgārjuna. Dordogne: Editions Padmakara, 2008.

A Torch Lighting the Way to Freedom. Dudjom Rinpoche, Jigdrel Yeshe Dorje. Boston: Shambhala, 2011.

Treasury of Precious Qualities, Book One. Longchen Yeshe Dorje, Kangyur Rinpoche. Boston: Shambhala, 2001. Revised version with root text by Jigme Lingpa, 2010.

Treasury of Precious Qualities, Book Two: Vajrayana and the Great Perfection. Longchen Yeshe Dorje, Kangyur Rinpoche. Boston: Shambhala, 2013.

The Way of the Bodhisattva (Bodhicharyavatara). Shantideva. Boston: Shambhala, 1997, 2006, 2008.

White Lotus. Jamgön Mipham. Boston: Shambhala, 2007.

The Wisdom Chapter: Jamgön Mipham's Commentary on the Ninth Chapter of "The Way of the Bodhisattva." Jamgön Mipham. Boulder: Shambhala, 2017.

Wisdom: Two Buddhist Commentaries. Khenchen Kunzang Pelden and Minyak Kunzang Sönam. Dordogne: Editions Padmakara, 1993, 1999.

The Wish-Fulfilling Jewel. Dilgo Khyentse. Boston: Shambhala, 1988.

The Words of My Perfect Teacher. Patrul Rinpoche. Sacred Literature Series of the International Sacred Literature Trust. New York: HarperCollins, 1994; 2nd ed. Lanham, MD: AltaMira Press, 1998; Boston: Shambhala, 1998; New Haven, CT: Yale University Press, 2010.

Zurchungpa's Testament. Zurchungpa and Dilgo Khyentse. Ithaca, NY: Snow Lion, 2006, 2020.

Khangsar Tenpa'i Wangchuk's Collected Works

In 2019, the Padmakara Translation Group began the project of translating the entire Collected Works of the Nyingma master Khangsar Tenpa'i Wangchuk under the guidance of Pema Wangyal Rinpoche and Jigme Khyentse Rinpoche, having received the transmission from Tenpa'i Wangchuk's nephew, Tsultrim Zangpo Rinpoche. The following is a list of volumes published to date. Several more are forthcoming.

The Natural Openness and Freedom of the Mind: A Treasure Tantra of the Great Perfection, by Deshek Lingpa and Khangsar Tenpa'i Wangchuk.
The Precious Treasury of the Fundamental Nature, by Longchenpa and Khangsar Tenpa'i Wangchuk.

INDEX

Anuyoga, 38
aperture of Brahmā, 168
appearances
  and awareness, evenness of, 100
  equality of, 11, 101–2
  examining, 7, 66, 67, 69
  exhaustion of, 39
  eyes and, 131
  in fourth state, 86–87
  as *hūṃ*, 59
  as kāyas and wisdoms, 13, 116
  lack of true existence of, 60
  manifesting, 5, 14, 46, 48, 70, 89,
    90, 117, 118
  mastery over, 20, 150, 161
  sealed by ultimate expanse, 124
  settling, 18, 155
  subsiding of, 21, 169
  See also under emptiness
appearances of spontaneous
    presence, 4, 40
  as one's own self-experience, 5,
    44–45, 192
  recognizing, 48
  unfolding of, 5, 43–44, 192
apprehending subject and
    apprehended object, 8, 48, 68,
    72, 74, 76, 84
approach and accomplishment
    practices, 119
Array of Studded Jewels Tantra,
    138–39
Atiyoga. *See* Great Perfection
attachment, 8, 53, 57, 74, 76, 107
attainments
  completing, 18, 149, 150
  three kinds, 20, 161–62, 198
avadhūtī, 130. *See also* central
    channel
aversion, 8, 53, 74, 76, 107
awareness, 143
  as buddha, 10, 96, 97–98
  as cognizant potency, 22, 170
  directed at evil person, 20,
    161–62
  as fourth state, 9, 85–89, 194

great equality of, 90–93, 195
and ground and path, inseparability
    of, 28–29
as ground of delusion, 46–47
luminosity and emptiness,
    blending into, 21, 166, 167, 175
maturity of, 142
and mind, distinguishing, 8,
    74–76, 194
motionlessness of, 18, 154
obscurations to, 12, 103, 105
openness and freedom of, 89–90,
    194
as Padmasambhava, 21, 164, 165
path of, 14, 117
preserving, 104, 195
self-arisen, 78, 86, 89
self-display of, 30, 177
slowing down in prison of space,
    124
three definite assertions about, 76
and three kāyas, relationship of, 9,
    80, 82–83, 194
while settling naturally, 10, 94–96,
    195
See also self-cognizing awareness;
    self-experience of awareness
awareness-emptiness, 58, 60

Bamda Thubten Gelek, xvi
bardo beings, 178–79, 205n85
bardo of ultimate reality, 20, 21–22,
    164, 169–70
  beginning of, various views on,
    170–71
  stages of dissolution in, 172–78
bardos, number of, 163–64. *See also*
    four bardos
bewilderment, 53, 75, 107
birth
  four kinds, 33, 180
  miraculous, 22, 178, 179, 180
  power over, 21, 166, 167
blessings, xii, xxvi, 58, 64
bliss, meditative experience of, 12,
    109–11, 147

resting in, 59
wisdom of, 176
dharmakāya, 68, 102, 112, 162
  arising of, 10, 98
  luminosity of, 20, 164, 165
  nature of, 9, 80, 82–83
  as only sphere, 9, 84, 85
  realizing, 94
  and rūpakāya, inseparability of,
    112
  three aspects of, 3, 30, 31–32
  and universal ground, difference
    between, 74–76
  wisdom mind of, 10, 91, 93
dharmatā, 28, 79, 102, 152. *See also*
  vision of dharmatā in reality
Diamond Cutter Sūtra, 97
Dilgo Khyentse Rinpoche, 201n1
Distinguishing Three Key Points
  (Jigme Lingpa), 75, 76
Dodrub Jigme Tenpa'i Nyima, 81
Dogabma Monastery, 201n2
Dogongma Monastery, 201n2
dreams, 19, 101, 156–57, 165
Drime Özer. *See* Longchenpa
dualistic apprehension, 47, 134–35
Dudjom Dorje, 57
Dudjom Lingpa, xxiii, 201n2
  on appearance and awareness, 86
  on awareness inside, 143
  on inner purification, 56
  on no meditation, 96
  on view and conduct, 108
Dzogchen. *See* Great Perfection

effort
  relying on, 94, 95–96, 97, 195
  in thögal, xxiii, 13, 40, 115–16, 196
effortlessness, xxiii, 4, 36–38, 40, 41,
  77–78, 185, 192
eight classes of spirits, commander
  of, 23, 183, 184
eight consciousnesses, 8, 74, 76,
  78, 87
eighty-four thousand collections of
  teachings, 36, 77, 81

Ekajaṭī, 23, 183, 184
empowerment of great light rays, 150
empowerments. *See* four
  empowerments
emptiness, 62, 177
  appearances and, 10, 90–93
  appearances transferred toward,
    18, 151–52
  in bardo of becoming, 180
  erroneous views of, 50
  as intrinsically luminous, 7, 66,
    69–70
  and luminosity, inseparability of,
    9, 31, 82, 84–85, 92, 103, 194
  See also great emptiness
emptiness-clarity, 48, 75
emptiness-luminosity, 70, 95
enlightenment
  manifest, 113, 116, 204n62
  in single lifetime, xxiii
  See also mind set on enlightenment
entourage, 18, 149, 150
  of disciples, 23
  perfection of, 3, 29, 30, 31–32, 33,
    34
  and teacher's mind, inseparability
    of, 23, 181, 199
equality, 93
  all-pervading expanse of, 11, 61,
    101–2, 195
  free of conceptual elaboration, 73
  See also great equality
essence-drops, 118, 134, 138
eyes
  channels of, 130
  of dharmatā, 122
  divine, 178, 180
  of elements, 117–18
  heat in, dispelling, 140
  impure and refined, 117–18
  motionlessness of, 18, 154
  pathway of, 14, 117, 118
  of sublime knowledge, 122, 132, 134
  of wisdom, 117–18, 122, 136
  See also lamp of far-catching water
    lasso

Ekajaṭī

Rāhula

Dorje Lekpa

Shenpa Marnak